CHURCH
DOESN'T END

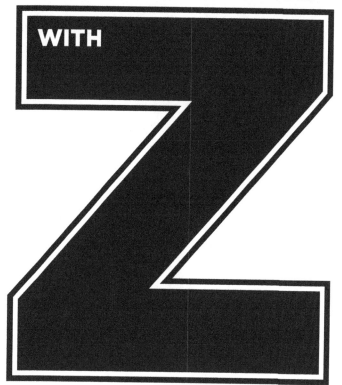

WITH

Z

CHURCH
DOESN'T END

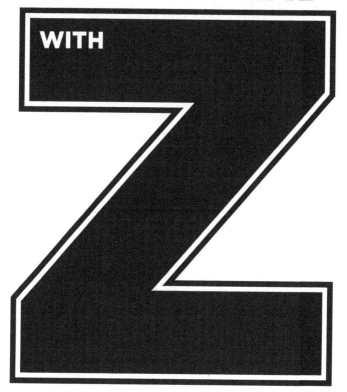

WITH

Z

WHY GEN Z IS LEAVING THE CHURCH
AND HOW TO REACH THEM

REESE CARLSON

Book Credits:
Cover Design by Julie Csizmadia
Photography by Bethlehem Kennington
Editing by Marty Hohmann

CONTENTS

INTRODUCTION. VII

PART I: THE MODERN MOMENT

CHAPTER 1: WE'RE NOT IN KANSAS ANYMORE. 3

CHAPTER 2: INTRODUCING Z 9

CHAPTER 3: THE INTERSECTION OF CHURCH AND CULTURE. 25

CHAPTER 4: REVERSING CULTURE—BACK TO KANSAS? 43

CHAPTER 5: THE CONVERSATION STARTS WITH US 57

PART II: REACHING GEN Z

CHAPTER 6: LITTLE RASCALS AND HORROR MOVIES. 73

CHAPTER 7: SYSTEM STUDENTS 87

CHAPTER 8: BE REAL, BRO 107

CHAPTER 9: THE PRESENT IS KING. 127

CHAPTER 10: HURT 141

CHAPTER 11: A CATALYST CALLED DOUBT 157

CHAPTER 12: KILLING THE BRAND 167

CHAPTER 13: ENGAGING ~~CONSUMERS~~ CREATORS. 185

CHAPTER 14: CHANGES 205

CHAPTER 15: THE FUTURE CHURCH 213

ACKNOWLEDGMENTS. 221

ENDNOTES 223

INTRODUCTION

This book was born out of a burden.

A few years ago, I was burdened by the fact that so many young people leave the church after they graduate high school. This burden came about after seeing members of my own church leave, alongside statistics that identified this growing epidemic. Each year, I watched as young people burned out on Christianity just as fast as they caught on fire in the first place. As a youth pastor, this was discouraging and disheartening.

Why are so many young people leaving the church? What do we need to do differently in order to reach this next generation with the Gospel?

I quickly began reading everything I could get my hands on concerning Generation Z and their exit from the church. What I found was a significant amount of research, but a lack of practical ways for churches to understand Gen Z and actually implement new ministry techniques to address the disconnect between Gen Z and the church.

This prompted a desire to help build a bridge between Gen Z and the church. As a member of Gen Z myself, there seems to be a significant disconnect between these two parties. The church doesn't understand Gen Z and Gen Z does not understand the church. The church is trying to "reach" young people, but the methods of evangelism feel like methods used to reach millennials and Gen Xers, not Gen Zers. And many of the methods we use—our language, ministries, programs, teachings—seem like they were created for "Christian America," which we have long since exited. As a current youth pastor, I believe we need a more robust understanding of Gen Z for those who are doing the work of ministry.

My aim in writing this book is to discover *why* Gen Z is leaving the church and *how* the church can reach this generation. But my other aim is simply to give hope. After considering a variety of titles for the book, my wife and I decided to move toward something that would encourage and inspire. Instead of a book title that focused on the problem (Gen Z leaving the church), we wanted to focus on the hope that God has for His church. It's a hope found in Jesus' words to Peter:

> **And I tell you, you are Peter, and on this rock I will build my church, and the gates of hell shall not prevail against it.**[1]

Not hell, nor secularism, nor atheism, not even a new generation, will prevail against the church. The church is the hope of the world for Gen Z as it was for all generations before it. So, my prayer is that this book gives you practical ways to reach Gen Z with the Gospel, along with some added encouragement that God's church is *still* the hope of the world.

THE BREAKDOWN

All of these burdens, questions, and hopes prompted me to launch an in-depth examination of Generation Z and the state of the church in America. A significant portion of this research was conducted during my time as a seminary student at Western Seminary.

The first section of this book sets the stage for our conversation about Gen Z and the church. It takes a look at the state of Christianity in America along with an introduction to Gen Z. I also spend a few chapters outlining how the church should think about culture, as the relationship between church and the surrounding culture is an important topic when it comes to ministering to specific people groups like Generation Z.

The second section of the book starts diving into the reasons why Gen Z is leaving the church along with specific characteristics that define Gen Z. Throughout each chapter I also share some ways that the church can address the reasons young people are leaving, along with some practical application.

And finally, the third section looks at the future of the church in America and how the church can implement new strategies.

RESEARCH

The research conducted for this project was a synthesis of studies by groups like Barna, Pew Research, and Lifeway. I should note there are many challenges the church is facing that I did not include for various reasons. For example, technology is hardly mentioned in this book, partly because so much has already been written on Gen Z's relationship with technology. I am aiming at the *main reasons* why Gen Z is leaving the church, which will of course leave out some of the other reasons. Some of the causes for leaving may be the same as previous generations, but many are completely unique to Gen Z.

When conducting research, it is important to recognize that statistics are helpful, but they don't tell the entire story. Just because someone marks "Christian" on a poll does not necessarily mean they are a Christian. There are difficulties in interpreting such numbers, especially with cultural Christianity on the decline. Statistics were an important aspect of my research, but we must keep in mind that the polling system isn't perfect. Another danger of statistics is that we utilize numbers to "box people in," as if the person is entirely represented by a number. This can be the tendency when looking at generations as a whole. We should be reminded that each percentage point, each number, represents a human who has a unique story which cannot be described within the confines of a number.

Finally, my desire is that this book will serve as both an inspiration and a tool for you to reach young people for Jesus more effectively. Whether you are a parent, pastor, teacher, or simply someone who wants to see young people fall in love with Jesus, I hope we can unite around the mission of reaching the next generation for Christ. We are far better together than we are apart.

PART 1:

THE
MODERN
MOMENT

CHAPTER 1

WE'RE NOT IN **KANSAS** **ANYMORE**

In the 1939 movie, *The Wizard of Oz*, Dorothy slowly opens up a door, looks outside, and says, "Toto, I have a feeling we're not in Kansas anymore."[1]

Alright. I'm going to be honest. I've never even seen *The Wizard of Oz*.

But this goes to show just how well-known this phrase has become. The quote has been used countless times throughout the years to illustrate what is not normal or stepping out into the unfamiliar and uncomfortable.

In many ways, this phrase illustrates where America is as a country today.

Here in the United States, we have undergone a dramatic shift from "faith at the center" of culture to "faith at the margins" of culture.

What was once typical and expected—going to church on Sunday, praying at school, a Bible on the nightstand—is now unfamiliar and atypical. What used to be the norm is now the exception.

The phrase "I have a feeling America isn't Christian anymore" would be a valid expression for people of faith today.

In the 1950s, the U.S. population underwent its biggest "boom" in history—from 150 million in 1950 to 180 million in 1960—hence the name baby boomer generation.[2]

In response to the population explosion, churches and schools expanded, and organized religion thrived.

Here's a crazy statistic:

> **On a typical Sunday morning from 1955-58, almost HALF of all Americans were attending church. While half of Americans were attending church on a Sunday morning, those who reported they *belonged* to a church was over 70%.[3]**

We like to think of the 18th and 19th centuries as a time when just about everyone went to church. We picture the colonists and founders of our nation living in a time when church attendance was as common as going to school.

But the period of the 1950s surpassed the church attendance of these previous "Christendom" centuries.[4]

In the 1950s, church attendance in America was at its peak. Today, it is at its lowest point.

In 2021, a study was released that found church attendance in America had reached its lowest percentage of all time: 47% percent reported belonging to a church or religious institution.[5]

It should be noted that we are talking about *church attendance,* not *Christianity* as a whole. The number of those who identify as "Christian" is decreasing as well, but this is partly due to cultural Christians no longer checking a box for religious affiliation.[6]

The transition from America as a "Christian nation" to a secular, post-Christian society happened almost overnight.

The number of people who reported belonging to a church held steady at around 70% from the 1950s until 1999. But from 2000 to 2021, attendance plummeted more than 20%. This dramatic shift in church attendance is a rapid decline for a relatively short period of just 20 years.[7]

Typically, we see cultural values and societal norms shift rather slowly from generation to generation. But in the last 20 years, the advancement of computers, smartphones, and social media has caused information to be transmitted at a significantly higher rate than before.

The result? A rapidly changing culture with distinct generational differences.

While we can identify differences between the baby boomer generation and Gen X, the differences are not *nearly* as extreme as the differences between millennials and Gen Z.[8]

Why?

Technological advancements in the '90s and 2000s propelled the rate of cultural change. The invention of the internet, iPhone, and social media all contributed to this cultural acceleration.

Think about it.

During the 1960s, the information people had to wait to read about in the paper the next day, they could now see on the nightly news. Fast forward, and what we used to have to wait for on the nightly news can now be read by hopping on the internet. Now, what we used to have to jump on the computer to see can quickly be acquired on the device in our pocket.

In their book, *The Acceleration of Cultural Change*, authors Bentley and O'Brien outline this significant acceleration of culture through the advancement of technology.[9]

The speed at which we have been able to transmit and receive information is just one of the many reasons we have seen culture accelerate over the last 20 years.

And with this acceleration came many things, but notably the sharp decrease in church attendance. So just like that, we're not in Kansas anymore.

But unlike the movie, we cannot close our eyes, click our heels three times, think, "there's no place like home," and return to the normal, familiar, and comfortable.[10]

We cannot rewind to "The good old days," where Christianity permeated every corner of the U.S. We are living in post-Christian America.

This is our new reality.

In response to this cultural change, I want to pose a question:

Are we preparing young people to follow Jesus in a world that no longer exists?

Are we teaching young people how to live in Kansas, although we are definitely not in Kansas anymore?

Are we teaching Generation Z how to follow Jesus in Christendom instead of teaching them how to follow Jesus in post-Christendom?

The Barna Group, an evangelical-based research organization, relates our current cultural moment to that of Daniel in the Old Testament.

When Daniel and other Hebrew elites were taken captive and placed into Babylon, their worldview changed entirely. In their book, *Gen Z: The Culture, Beliefs, and Motivations Shaping the Next Generation*, Barna states:

> **In order to remain faithful to their calling as the people of God, they had to adjust to a new reality. They had to reimagine what it meant to practice Judaism in a world where the Temple— the epicenter of their religious practice—no longer existed. They had to rethink their own**

story to re-examine their understanding of their place in the world and in God's intentions for creation. In response to a worldview-shifting calamity, prophets arose to equip God's people to live in a new world.[11]

Barna's summary statement:

"Are we making disciples for Jerusalem when we need to be making disciples for Babylon?"[12]

This is the question that all teachers, parents, pastors, and leaders need to be asking themselves.

In a culture that no longer reflects the values of Jesus, how do we lead, train, and disciple our young people to follow Jesus?

Before we think through the practicalities of uniquely and intentionally discipling Generation Z, let's jump into what we know about Generation Z today.

CHAPTER 2

INTRODUCING Z

So, if Jesus is the same yesterday, today, and forever, why is it important that we talk about generational differences?

First of all, Scripture recognizes the concept of generations.

The book of Acts recalls,

> **David, after he had served the purpose of God in his own *generation*, fell asleep and was buried.**[1]

This statement indicates that God has unique plans for each generation, just as He did with David.

Psalm 78 says,

> **My people, hear my teaching; listen to the words of my mouth. I will open my mouth with a parable; I will utter hidden things, things from**

of old—things we have heard and known, things our ancestors have told us. We will not hide them from their descendants; we will tell the next *generation* the praiseworthy deeds of the Lord, His power, and the wonders He has done.[2]

Psalm 78 is another example that illustrates that God's eternal purposes are accomplished in time, by and through each generation.

As pastor Benjamin Karuhije wrote,

> This reality demands that Christians, especially pastors and leaders, seek to understand not only the purposes of God, but the generations in which they have been placed—and how these two dynamics interact.[3]

If generations matter to God, which means it's important for us to understand each generation, who is Generation Z, exactly?

Generally speaking, Gen Z includes those born between 1995 and 2010.[4] So if you are serving in youth ministry, there are no longer any millennials in your youth group. Grades 6-12 are now entirely made up of Gen Z, with Generation Alpha close behind them.

Gen Z grew up with cell phones, had an Instagram page before they started high school, and do not remember a time before the internet. By the time the iPhone came out in 2007, the oldest Gen Zers were 12 years old—just entering middle school. For members of Gen Z, their entire adolescence has been marked by the all-powerful Apple™ icon. The influence of the internet is why sociologist Jean Twenge dubbed Gen Z "iGen."[5]

Generation Z is now the largest age group in terms of population, and half of this population is non-white, making it the most ethnically diverse generation in American history.[6] The world Gen Z has grown up in has been somewhat tumultuous. They grew up during the Great Recession of 2008, where many saw their family struggle financially. Additionally, Gen Z grew up in a post-9/11 world, where the U.S. has been at war since most of them were born. Their growing-up years are marked by some of the deadliest natural disasters worldwide (2004 Indian Ocean tsunami; 2010 Haiti earthquake; 2011 Japan earthquake and tsunami).

Feed Youth Ministry shares what effect such events have had on Gen Z:

> **As with each generation, Gen Zers faced a unique set of world events that have shaped their generational psyche and influenced how they see the world. Much of what Gen Z witnessed has taught them that the world is uncertain and possibly unsafe.[7]**

One of the outcomes of exposure to the Great Recession is that Gen Z is more financially conservative than their millennial predecessors. Twelve percent of Gen Z says they have already begun saving for retirement. Many members of Gen Z desire stable jobs with good pay over careers that "make them happy."[8] Millennials are often known for pursuing happiness in their careers, even at the cost of their financial stability.[9] However, Gen Z takes a more financially driven approach in their job endeavors.

Gen Z is called *iGen* because of the influence of the internet, but there is another "I" word that drives this nickname. The rise of *individualization* shapes the way Gen Z thinks, feels, and behaves. This is what makes Gen Z different from every previous generation. Jean Twenge describes what makes Gen Z so unique:

> They socialize in completely new ways, reject once sacred social taboos, and want different things from their lives and careers. They are obsessed with safety and fearful of their economic futures, and they have no patience for in- equality based on gender, race, or sexual orientation. They are at the forefront of the worst mental health crisis in decades, with rates of teen depression and suicide skyrocketing since 2011. Contrary to the prevalent idea that children are growing up faster than previous generations did, iGen'ers are growing up more slowly: 18-year-olds now act like 15-year-olds used to, and 13-year-olds like 10-year-olds. Teens are physically safer than ever, yet they are more mentally vulnerable.[10]

As you can see, Gen Z is tough to nail down. Throwing out statistics to explain this diverse generation is helpful, but incomplete. Each member of Gen Z is different and expresses themselves in unique ways, which is why it's important to remember that statistics represent general tendencies, not universal norms.

As a youth pastor who is actually a member of Gen Z, there are many ways I relate to the students in my youth group. Still, there are many ways where I feel incredibly disconnected (I often feel like I need a translator when speaking to 9th-grade boys).

The rapid transmission of media and constantly developing culture create the fluid generation we call "Gen Z." We sometimes feel like we have Gen Z figured out, and then they say, "Bet. Watch me yeet this squirrel." And then we're back to square one.

While we will expand on the cultural values of Gen Z later on, the above characteristics serve as a brief starting point for understanding Gen Z. These traits will be important to keep in mind as we talk about how the church can engage this unique generation.

THE EXODUS OF Z

We've already talked about the declining numbers in church attendance here in the U.S. While we often define non-believers as atheist or agnostic, there is a similar category that many members of Gen Z would place themselves in. This category is called "The Religious Nones."

Those categorized as a religious "none" say their religion is "nothing in particular." This group now makes up 23% of the U.S. population. The rise in religious nones represents a sharp increase from 2007 (the last time Pew Research conducted such a study) when 16% of Americans were religious nones. And more specifically, religious nones make up the highest percentage of young people.[11]

Pew Research notes, "Overall, religiously unaffiliated people are more concentrated among young adults than other age groups."[12]

The self-reported "religious none" category represents a movement away from traditional religious affiliations. While a millennial may use a term like "atheist" to distinguish themselves from the religious, the children of these millennials, Gen Z, are so far removed from religiosity that they seem to reject religious labels altogether. Checking "Christian" on a poll may have been the norm, but now it's more acceptable to just put nothing.

But the most shocking statistic of all is the "70%" number.

If you've been around youth ministry at all or the church in general, you've probably heard of it (and like me, maybe you're tired of hearing it).

Over the years, the percentage of churchgoing high schoolers who leave the church after they graduate has fluctuated. In recent years, the number has been as low as 50% and as high as 70%. But the number people usually think of when they talk about the vast group of young people leaving the church is the big 70% number.[13]

According to a 2017 Lifeway Research study, 66 % of American young adults who attended a Protestant church regularly for at least a year as a teenager say they also dropped out for at least a year between ages 18 and 22.[14]

But don't many of these people come back to the church in their later years?

Yes. Some do. Out of those who leave the church between the ages of 18 and 22, 31% report later attending church regularly. This 31% represents a small glimmer of hope in an otherwise depressing statistic.

Ben Trueblood, director of student ministry at Lifeway, recognizes this in saying,

> **On some level, we can be encouraged that some return. While at the same time, we should recognize that when someone drops out in these years, there is a 69% chance they will stay gone.**[15]

Just because a young person leaves the church doesn't mean they are gone forever. If we know anything from Scripture, we know God uses unlikely means to reach unlikely people.[16] Nobody is too far gone for God.

However, the goal of this book is to assess the problem of young people *leaving* the church. We will keep in mind that some do return, but the fact that many *do not* is enough to cause concern.

Not only is this 70% statistic significant, but it's also alarming.

If you care about young people, or the state of Christianity in America, or if you are simply a follower of Jesus, the reality that two out of every three churchgoing teenagers are leaving the church when they graduate is disheartening.

If you are a church leader or specifically a youth leader, you are probably tired of hearing about this statistic.

You are probably tired of people reminding you that the students you pour your heart and soul into will leave the very thing you are calling them to.

You are probably tired of seeing student after student fall in love with Jesus, only to eventually leave the community that brought them into that love for Jesus.

Or, maybe you are tired of well-intentioned people who have no investment in youth ministry whatsoever telling you what *you* should be doing differently to change that 70% number (This has *never* happened to me, of course...).

Or maybe you are just tired. Period.

Whatever your position may be, I know I am tired of this statistic, mainly because of the fear this number causes in churches, parents, and pastors. The result is constant finger-pointing at various culprits for the cause of the 70% statistic, as well as the reluctance of *the church* to accept responsibility and make corporate shifts in the way we think about church and discipling young people.

All of this frustration led me to do something about this problem.

I've been conducting an independent study at Western Seminary alongside youth ministry extraordinaire, Dr. Ron Marrs, to examine the 70% statistic on a deeper level. I sought to answer two main questions.

First, why are so many young people leaving the church?

And second, what should the local church's response be in light of such findings?

In this book, I have laid out the discoveries which have been helpful in my youth ministry context, and I hope they will be beneficial to you as well.

LEAVING CHURCH, LOVING JESUS

I recently talked with a young person who used to be in my youth group. He confided in me that he was going through a painful season because of a new development in his personal life. And the majority of the pain was caused by the response of the Christian community around him.

As I listened to his story, it seemed as though the last few months had been excruciatingly painful and borderline traumatic. I began to wonder if he would leave the church for good, like so many other Christians his age.

When I asked him what kind of impact this experience had on his faith, he responded, "I feel further away from the church than ever before, but closer to Jesus."

As I heard this, tears began to well up in my eyes. I think I started to cry for two reasons.

First, I cried because of the painful experience caused by followers of Jesus. The same community that should be loving and supporting our young people drove him to a deep place of hurt.

I cried because *this* was the realization that so many young people have in the church today. They are sick of institutionalized religion and the judgment that sometimes comes with this institution. So they leave. And I saw it happening right before me.

Second, I cried because of the beauty and radical love of Jesus. Only He could take someone who has fallen out of love with the church, who has felt unloved by the very people who profess to love Jesus, and bring him to a deeper and more meaningful relationship with Him.

For my friend, he expressed that although he felt pain from the Christian community, he felt the comfort and love of God. He felt the acceptance of his creator during a moment where he felt anything *but* accepted.

I was shocked that this student was turned off by the church but somehow still pursued a relationship with Jesus.

Leaving the church but loving Jesus. How could this be?

For many young people who grow up in church, "leaving the church but loving Jesus" would resonate with their story as well.

In 2017, Barna created a metric to capture those who most neatly fit this description.[17]

This metric includes those who self-identify as Christian and who strongly agree that their religious faith is "very important" in their life but are "de-churched."

"De-churched" means they have "attended church in the past but haven't done so in the last six months (or more)." These individuals have a sincere faith but are notably absent from church.

According to Barna, this group makes up 10% of the population and is a segment that continues to grow.[18] Additionally, out of the 66% of young people who said they left the church, only 10% said they dropped out because they stopped believing in God.[19]

An article from Inter-Faith Youth Core titled "Gen Z is Keeping the Faith. Just Don't Expect to See Them at Worship" recognizes this trend in a recent 2021 study:

> When asked to rate their trust of organized religion on a 10-point scale, 63% of young people answered 5 or below, including 52% of those who say they're affiliated with a religious tradition. You read that right: Over half of young people who claim a religious affiliation have little trust in the very religious institutions with which they identify.[20]

The bottom line?

> The question is not whether Gen Zers are going to abandon religious institutions—they're already well on their way. The question is whether faith leaders will walk alongside them as they encounter the divine in new ways.[21]

But I want to pose the question, is this ok?

Is it ok that Gen Z is leaving the church but still following Jesus?

My answer would be no; it's not.

Of course, for my friend, it is entirely understandable why he would want to leave the church. And I would much rather have him leave the church and still follow Jesus than abandon his faith altogether.

But should our response to the growing segment of people who are leaving the church but loving Jesus be, "Well, that's not a big deal, because they are still Christians?"

I don't think so.

Because it *is* a big deal.

When someone becomes a Christian, they have been brought into a right relationship with God by the saving work through Jesus Christ. We read in 2 Corinthians 5 that:

> **God was in Christ reconciling the world to Himself, not counting their trespasses against them, and He has committed to us the word of reconciliation.**[22]

But that's not all.

Being a Christian not only means being reconciled to God but being reconciled to one another.

Removing God from His rightful place as King also involves a break in fellowship with our brother and sister.

The reconciliation we receive by the work of Jesus on the cross is twofold: We are reconciled to our maker—God, and we are reconciled to His image-bearers—our neighbor.

> For He Himself is our peace, who has made the two one and has destroyed the barrier, the dividing wall of hostility... His purpose was to create in Himself one new man out of the two, thus making peace, and in this one body to reconcile both of them to God through the cross, by which He put to death their hostility.[23]

Mark Dever, the senior pastor of Capitol Hill Baptist Church in Washington, D.C., and president of 9Marks, examines the possibility of being a Christian apart from belonging to a church community.

> In short, it's impossible to answer the question "what is a Christian?" without ending up in a conversation about the church; at least, in the Bible it is. Not only that, it's hard to stick with just one metaphor for the church because the New Testament uses so many of them: a family and a fellowship, a body and a bride, a people and a temple, a lady and her children. And never does the New Testament conceive of the Christian existing on a prolonged basis outside the fellowship of the church.[24]

Can a Christian exist apart from the church?

Can an NFL player exist apart from a team?

Not really. Picture this.

"So, you play in the NFL?" "Yep."

"What team are you on?" "Well, I'm not on a team." "..."

Yeah. That doesn't really work.

Pastor and Author Rich Villodas wrote:

> **The Bible is more communal than individual. Jesus teaches us to pray 'Our Father' not 'My Father.' Paul uses the phrase 'Our Lord' 53 times and 'My Lord' only one time. 'Jesus is my personal savior' is not found in Scripture. We are the people of God. We belong to each other.**[25]

We know that we are saved by our faith in Jesus Christ; there's no doubt about that.[26]

In our Western individualism, we have made "my personal relationship with Jesus" (a phrase not found in the Bible, by the way) the barometer for faithfulness to Christ.

And while personal faith in Christ *is* important, the New Testament would not have understood following Jesus apart from the community of believers—the church.

So back to the question. Leaving the church but loving Jesus.

Are we ok with this?

And by "we," I mean followers of Jesus, church leaders, and parents.

And by "Ok," I mean are we content with those who leave the church, even if they do profess to be a Christian? Do we believe this is God's intention for His people? And do we believe this is the best way to live out one's faith vibrantly?

I'm hoping your answer is no.

But we are not only going to be looking at those who leave the church and keep their faith. We will also be examining those young people who have abandoned the church *along* with their faith altogether.

If you are reading this, I'm guessing you care about the epidemic of young people walking away from the church. And I'm thinking that you probably even have a personal relationship with one of these young people. And I'm willing to bet that you would want to know why they left the church and if there was anything *your* church could have done differently to keep this from happening. Me too.

If this is the case, we need to discover why young people are leaving the church and re-think how we can engage Generation Z with the Gospel.

If we want to understand how to minister to Gen Z effectively, we must first seek to understand their culture; in other words, the things that define Gen Z.

But how, exactly, should the church engage with the surrounding culture?

CHAPTER 3

THE INTERSECTION OF **CHURCH** AND **CULTURE**

"Why even talk about culture? The Gospel message can stand on its own."

This statement is one I have heard rather frequently in church circles.

If we are going to be committed to the Gospel message, I think the question, "Should we even be talking about culture?" is actually worth asking.

My answer is an overt "YES." But let's back up.

What is culture, and why should it matter to the church?

> We use the term 'culture' to refer to the common ideas, feelings, and values that guide community and personal behavior that organize and regulate what the group thinks, feels, and does about God, the world, and humanity.[1]

This definition from author and professor Harvie Conn explains why culture is so influential:

> Culture guides what a group thinks, feels, and does about God, the world, and humanity.[2]

Think about it like this: Fish don't know they're in water. If you tried to explain it, they'd say, "Water? What's water?" They're so surrounded by it that it's impossible to see. They can't see it until they jump outside of it.

In many ways, culture is like the water fish swim in. We are so enveloped in it that we don't even realize the extent which we are shaped by it. If we don't zoom out and examine our surrounding culture, it's difficult to discern the ways in which culture is shaping our beliefs and practices.

If the surrounding culture here in the U.S. is guiding our thoughts and feelings about God, then it is worth exploring what this culture is guiding us toward and how we can share the Gospel in a way that makes sense to the culture of Gen Z.

A Gospel message disconnected from culture may be heard, but not received.

For example, whenever Alison and I go to Seattle to watch a Mariners game, there is always a guy standing on a platform with a megaphone. I'm guessing you've probably run across something similar.

He shouts things like, "Jesus died for your sins, repent or perish!" Or "A man who lies with a man is an abomination to God!" While this may make you cringe, let's try to approach this method of evangelism objectively.

In the most basic sense, are the things this man saying true? Well, yes. We can find these statements in Scripture.

But do you think anyone is actually going to *receive* what he is saying? Probably not. His tactics are likely confirming the negative opinions many already have about Christianity.

So, what's wrong with this man's message if he simply says what's in the Bible?

Not only does it lack any sense of love, but it is disconnected from culture. People are hearing, but not receiving.

In a previous culture, this method of evangelism may have been more successful. When absolute truth reigned supreme, the presentation of that truth wasn't as important.

But in our day and age, the presentation of truth is almost as important as the message itself.

Most of the time, people don't care if what you're saying is true if it's unkind, offensive, or inauthentic.

So back to the question. If the Gospel can stand on its own, why do we need to understand culture?

The Gospel can stand on its own. But why wouldn't we do our best to help others understand and receive the Gospel?

Not only is such an approach practical (in that it helps people comprehend the Gospel), but it's biblical.[3]

Throughout his ministry, the Apostle Paul communicated the Gospel message so that specific cultures could understand it. He famously declared:

> To the Jews I became as a Jew, in order to win Jews. To those under the law I became as one under the law (though not myself being under the law) that I might win those under the law. To those outside the law I became as one outside the law (not being outside the law of God but under the law of Christ) that I might win those outside the law. To the weak I became weak, that I might win the weak. I have become all things to all people, that by all means I might save some. I do it all for the sake of the Gospel, that I may share with them in its blessings.[4]

Paul identified with the people he was trying to reach. He adapted his lifestyle to theirs in any place that might hinder them from hearing the Gospel. He valued the Gospel more than his own rights, more than his own comfort, more than his own culture. If there was any offense in his presentation of the Gospel, he wanted it to be the offense of the cross, not the offense of foreignness.[5]

Ed Stetzer, Executive Director of the Billy Graham Center at Wheaton College, explains Paul's method:

> Paul intentionally addressed his Jewish listeners one way but addressed pagan philosophers differently. When he addressed Jews, Paul began with Scripture. When he addressed Gentiles, he started with general revelation. The focus of Paul's sermons remained the same—the Gospel. However, Paul shifted his presentation of the Gospel to fit the worldviews of his listeners.[6]

Paul was able to adapt his evangelistic approach based on who he was speaking to, which is partly why he was such an effective communicator of the Gospel. The process of sharing the Gospel so the listener can understand and receive it is called *contextualization.*

Contextualization can be defined as:

> A tool to enable, insofar as it is humanly possible, an understanding of what it means that Jesus Christ, the Word, is authentically experienced in each and every human situation.[7]

A more straightforward definition of contextualization:

> The process of making the Gospel and the church as much at home as possible in a given cultural context.[8]

And really, this is what we are trying to do here in this book. What is the culture of Gen Z, and how can we "make the Gospel at home" for this specific culture?

We will be more effective in forming members of Generation Z into communities of mature disciples of Jesus if we adapt our methods to maximize the opportunities and overcome the challenges they face by virtue of their shared generational traits.[9]

PHILOSOPHY OF CULTURE

How did the early church maintain consistent growth in a time when Christianity held zero cultural or political power? In the first three centuries, followers of Jesus carved out a path of faithfulness to God despite having fewer religious liberties than we have today. And the early church didn't just survive. *It thrived.*

How?

Reflecting on the early church, Whitworth University professor Gerald Sittser writes,

> The success of the early church was certainly not inevitable. Christians could have accommodated to the culture to win recognition and approval, which would have undermined the uniqueness of their belief system and way of life. Or Christians could have isolated themselves from the culture to hide and survive, which would have kept them on the margins—safe, to be sure, but also irrelevant.[10]

Instead of being consumed by culture or retreating from culture, followers of Jesus fostered a *third way.* The secret to the explosion of the early church was not cultural relativism or cultural escapism, but rather a Jesus centeredness that infused culture with the hope and love of Christ.

Today, whenever the conversation between the church and culture arises, there is a tendency to lean to one extreme or the other.

The church often adopts a *consumed by culture* or *retreat from culture* mindset.

But if we want to follow in the footsteps of the early church— which thrived under little cultural or political acceptance—we need to embody the *third way.*

This third option understands that culture doesn't dictate the beliefs and practices of the church, nor should culture be utterly absent from the church. The third option is a church that speaks prophetically to culture. In the third option, the church understands the culture and signals to the world that there is a different way to be human. Lastly, and most importantly, the third way places Jesus at the very center of its mission.

Tim Keller explains the impact culture has on us today,

> **We are social-cultural beings, and our inner-heart motivations are profoundly shaped by the human communities in which we are embedded.**[11]

A Gospel message that lacks cultural awareness or cultural application will cause people to struggle to understand how this

Gospel is relevant to their lives today. After all, for many members of Gen Z, they leave the church not for lack of faith but a lack of relevancy. They don't see how church speaks to their life in the here and now. A Gospel-centered church with cultural awareness communicates that Christianity is not only a possible option, but that it is a desperate necessity.

If we recognize that each generation has new values and characteristics, the church should consider adapting its practices to meet each generation with these unique characteristics.

There is a fine line here, however.

CONSUMED BY CULTURE

The idea that the church must adapt, shift, and change in order to reflect and attract the culture is a dangerous idea and a slippery slope towards an irrelevant church.

Wait, but how could being relevant actually make the church irrelevant?

The church becomes irrelevant when it focuses *more* on cultural relevancy than Gospel transformation. A church that proclaims "Jesus is the hope of the world" will be relevant to those who are looking for hope. And people are *always* looking for hope.

While we want to engage the world around us and provide meaningful ways for people to connect their lives to the Gospel, there is also danger in letting a new generation dictate the practices of the church. The reality is, young people want to be part of something *different from culture*.

When church just becomes a reflection of the world around it, it ceases to be the church and fails to provide an alternative way of living.

Cultural commentator and pastor Mark Sayers identifies this phenomenon as "The Disappearing Church"—where the church blends in with the rest of the world.[12]

The church has been and always will be countercultural.

As James writes,

> **Whoever therefore wants to be a friend of the world makes himself an enemy of God.[13]**

When we try to conform the Gospel to look more like the world, we dilute the Gospel into a light and fluffy story that doesn't require anything of us. What young person would want to be part of this sort of Gospel? The Gospel is daring. The Gospel is revolutionary. The Gospel invites us into a new way of living, a new reality. It's so much more than we often make it out to be.

Author Shane Claiborne once said,

> **If we lose our kids to a culture of drugs, alcohol, and partying, it isn't because we didn't entertain them. It's because we didn't challenge them. We didn't dare them.[14]**

I believe that young people want to be challenged to participate in something bigger than themselves.

As a youth pastor, I try to think of the next fun activity for our youth group gathering or the next big event that will draw kids in. But ultimately, the church can't compete with Hollywood.

We can't compete with the best show in town, whether it be an NBA game or a concert. But we do have something to offer that those agencies and the rest of the world can't:

The best news of all time.

The news is that there is a God who believes you were worth dying for and that He desires a relationship with you. And that this relationship involves the most incredible mission in human history: The great (co)Mission.[15]

We are challenged with taking the Gospel to the ends of the Earth, teaching people the ways of Jesus, and participating in God's Kingdom work here on Earth, so that broken lives will be restored and that God's glory will be magnified throughout all of creation. This is a message worth coming to hear and a mission worth partaking in.

We should be careful not to get so caught up in the culture around us that we end up just offering an additional entertainment option that happens on Sunday mornings. Conversely, we should seek to be the physical embodiment of hope for a broken world like Christ called us to be.

Being so "culturally relevant" that the church is consumed by culture is, of course, NOT the function of the church. We should be in the world, but not of it.[16]

We stand on the unchanging Word of God, which means our theology and mission should not change. How we carry out this mission, however, does and should change.

And in many ways, the culture around us has changed, but the church hasn't adapted its ministry philosophies to engage this new generation. Many of us are operating as if we are still in Kansas while the culture has long since moved on, resulting in the perception that the church is completely irrelevant.

This is one of the many reasons I believe a generation is growing up who doesn't want anything to do with the church.

RETREAT FROM CULTURE

"It's our job just to preach the Gospel. If they don't get it, that's their fault."

This sentiment may ring true for those who adopt a "retreat from culture" perspective.

Historically, the church hasn't always conducted evangelism with consideration to the cultural influences of the audience.

In the Middle Ages, the Catholic Church in Rome believed that faith was lucid. In other words, exposure to the Gospel was sufficient for people to be transformed, regardless of the cultural context.

One common practice of the church was to compel Jews to listen to the preaching of the Gospel in the ghettos of Rome and Venice. In these ghettos, Jews were brought out to hear a teaching of the

Gospel where they were forced to listen. Shockingly, the Jews weren't very interested in hearing these messages.

They wanted to avoid hearing the preaching so severely that they stuffed cotton into their ears so they couldn't hear. This led the Catholic Church to assign proctors to inspect the people's ears and remove the cotton so they would listen to the message.[17]

Today, you don't see the church forcing people to listen to the Gospel in this manner, but this practice has been subliminally adopted throughout the church in many ways.

It's the idea that if people aren't receptive to the Gospel, it's their fault. Not ours. We tend to think it's the audience's problem, not the communicator's problem. But really, we should be asking the question, "How could I have communicated that in a way that makes sense to their culture?"

Many international missionaries are excellent in this practice, perhaps because they assume a foreign people group wouldn't process the Gospel message the same way they would. They understand that things like guilt, shame, fear, and power function uniquely from culture to culture.

And maybe that's part of the problem. We assume Gen Z receives information, processes new ideas, values history, responds to authority, etc., *in the same way as previous generations*. But this is far from the truth.

Remember, we are not in Kansas anymore. Christian America as we know it is extinct; we cannot expect methods of evangelism that worked 50 years ago to work the same way today.

The "Retreat from Culture" mindset is often born out of the growing secular culture and the Christian's disdain for it. When Christians see their country become less Christian in both the private and public sectors, there can be a tendency to fear culture and remove oneself from culture altogether.

Ed Stetzer comments:

> Some evangelicals mistakenly believe that Scripture's warnings against the world, the cosmos, are warnings against culture itself. However, this is not the case. All people are fashioned in the image of God and are recipients of common grace. This means that we should expect to find some positive features present in every culture, even non-Christian cultures. At the same time, every person has sinned, and we should expect to find some negative features present in every culture. Instead of shunning culture completely, we should instead engage culture with care and discernment.[18]

If we understand that Scripture isn't warning us against culture itself, we need to consider how the church can speak to our growing secular world. Unfortunately, our secular brothers and sisters are often stamped with a "Proceed with Caution" sign or a full-on "Road Closed. Use Detour" sign, which we, as the church, place on them. This attitude leads to a form of neglect and disdain for the rest of the world, ultimately isolating believers from non-believers entirely.

Back to Mark Sayers:

> A growing sense of worry haunts the Western church. The rise of a post-Christian society, alongside declining numbers of those who practice biblical faith, combined with a corresponding weakening of Christian influence, has created an anxious mood. This mood can range from a sense of defeat to a feeling of deep vulnerability to a desire to retreat into a religious refuge... Our fears are usually connected to the boogeyman we call secularism.[19]

When we take the sort of mentality that retreats from culture, not only does this make it difficult for the church to be the light in the darkness as we are called to be, but it inhibits young people from engaging with the church.

The "boogeyman of secularism," as Sayers says, drives Christians to believe that American Christendom as they know it is disappearing.

The typical evangelical response to this notion of oppression goes something like this: "We are the despised ones of our world. Things are being taken from us. Therefore, we must fight to defend it!"

The result of the growing disdain for our increasingly secular culture pushes Christians to feel like they need to defend God, which forms an "Us vs. Them" mentality. In my experience, this sort of mentality causes Gen Z to question the legitimacy of the

Christian church. Young people see us drawing lines and building walls where Jesus would be crossing these cultural boundaries.

The "Us vs. Them" attitude is where we currently find ourselves in this cultural moment.

Christians often view the people outside the church's walls as threats instead of neighbors to be loved. They are perceived as a threat because they may take the things so near and dear to us. And I am not suggesting that the "Us vs. Them" mentality is solely the responsibility of American Evangelicals. Certain aspects of secular postmodernism have sought to dismantle Christianity, such as the removal of God from places in the public sector: schools, businesses, politics, etc.

Defining secularism as "The Boogeyman," as Sayers puts it, is spot on.

Many evangelicals view secularism as the lurking, invisible force seeking to destroy everything Christians love and hold dear.

We might perceive secularism as a threat to the church, when it is often not. God will protect His church. And when the outside world seems to reject us, we must remember the church has always thrived when culture has marginalized and oppressed it, not when it has celebrated and embraced it.[20]

So, the extremes we can jump to are one, being consumed by culture, where the church ends up not looking significantly different from the culture around it. And two, retreating from culture, which views the surrounding culture as evil and doesn't engage the world with the Gospel.

My approach in this book will seek to build a sort of "middle ground" on the intersection of church and culture.

We want to understand the people who we are trying to reach. We want to understand their motivations and their characteristics. And we want to do everything we can to reach these people within their cultural context. At the same time, we want to offer something very different from the surrounding culture. While our churches may contextualize the Gospel in ways that make sense to a new generation, we will always stand on the truth of the Gospel and seek to engage people in a redemptive and prophetic manner that embodies Christ.

As Tim Keller put it,

> **Like Paul, we must invite and attract people through their culture's aspirations—calling them to come to Christ, the true wisdom and the true righteousness, the true power, the true beauty.**[21]

This methodology should be our aim as the local church.

We attract people through their culture's inclinations—calling them to the fullness of the Gospel of Jesus Christ. It is here—at the intersection of church and culture—that the Gospel is proclaimed both truthfully and relevantly to Gen Z.

REASONS FOR LEAVING:

- Church is perceived as irrelevant. It doesn't connect with the culture and values of Gen Z (*Retreating from Culture*).

- Church is perceived as a social club alternative. It doesn't offer anything different from the surrounding culture (*Consumed by Culture*).

STEPS FOR REACHING Z:

- Understand the cultural values of Gen Z. How can your church "make the Gospel at home" for members of Gen Z?

- Embody the counter-cultural Gospel. Prioritize the subversive ways of Jesus in services, programs, and ministries.

CHAPTER 4

REVERSING
CULTURE—
BACK TO KANSAS?

I'll never forget when I preached a message on the state of youth in America at our church. An older gentleman approached me when I came off stage after the third and final service. He thanked me for the message but wanted to highlight something that I didn't:

The Marxist regime taking Christ out of our nation.

He remarked that it all went downhill when they took prayer out of our schools in 1962. Since then, they have been forcing the LGBTQ agenda on our young people and corrupting our schools. They have been pumping young minds with the evils of Critical Race Theory. He left no doubt that the issue wasn't in the church, but the issue was the secular world. The fight was to be won not on the spiritual level or within the realm of the local church. No. The fight was to be won on the political and systemic level. If we change our systems and policies, if we get God back into the schools, if we stop talking about the LGBTQ agenda and remove Critical Race Theory, *then*, it seems, God will return to His throne in America.

After the man had finished, I felt sad.

I had tried to preach a message that was faithful to the Scriptures, that called the *church* to repentance, that convicted the hearts of God's people to faithfully disciple the next generation. I had tried to communicate the urgency of our cultural moment while also maintaining the sovereignty of our God, who is not surprised by the state of Christianity in our country. But above all of these things, I tried to tell the story of a God who had been faithful before and will be faithful again.

If our country had any hope left, it would be found in the person of Jesus. It would be found in humility, prayer, and repentance. Hope for our nation would not be found in imposing Christian values on the secular culture around us. It would be found in radically loving the neighbor in our secular culture and infusing that culture with the love of Jesus.

As American Christendom decreases, the desire to return to "life as it used to be" increases.

Like we discussed earlier, many have recognized that America looks significantly different than it did in the '50s, 60's and '70s. Faith used to be at the center of society, but now it is at the margins.

The phrase, "We're not in Kansas anymore" rings true for many Christians, but the problem is, we can't go back to Kansas.

While the desire for America to go back to the good old days doesn't seem harmful, this mindset may contribute to the church's lack of effort in engaging its surrounding culture.

Pete Williamson, a staff member at Intervarsity, an evangelical college campus ministry, shares the danger of this mindset.

> **Nostalgia for the past can play a part in people's wariness. I certainly mourn the decline of Christian identity wherever it is declining. But the church doesn't gain anything when we pine for some misremembered, bygone era when Christianity was (almost) the only shop in town.**[1]

We must remember and honor the past, especially times in history when God's Kingdom work was so widespread in our communities. Every Christian's faith depends on the inherited Christian tradition. But as theologian Gregory Jones points out, "Tradition is fundamentally different from traditionalism." He quotes the Yale historian Jaroslav Pelikan:

> **Tradition is the living faith of the dead; traditionalism is the dead faith of the living.**[2]

Traditionalism, where we long to return to the past by modeling a dead faith, inhibits our current mission. Going back in time is not an option.

While going back in time is not an option, retreating to areas of our country that *resemble* the past might be.

In my community south of Seattle, I have had numerous conversations with Christians considering moving to Idaho, Montana, or Texas—somewhere more politically and religiously conservative. Many of these conversations have been brought up because of growing concern over vaccines and other individual freedoms relating to COVID-19 and politics.

I recently heard a comment made by a pastor who lived in Southern California but has since moved to another state. He went as far as saying that he believes it is a sin for a Christian to live in this particular city.

Now, I cannot speak to the specifics of why someone may want to move to another part of the country, as each individual has his or her own personal reasons.

However, I have to wonder, what would happen if all the Christians moved out of our country's already more atheistic areas? What message would this send to our neighbors, and more importantly, what message would this communicate about our devotion to Christ and the sharing of His Kingdom?

Our senior pastor, Tung Le, recently encouraged our congregation to consider being the light to the culture God has called us into.

In the book of Jeremiah, the Israelites had just been exiled out of Jerusalem—a nation where God was honored and respected, to Babylon—a country that worshipped pagan gods with widespread immorality.[3]

And how does God want the Israelites to proceed?

> **Build houses and settle down; plant gardens and eat what they produce. Marry and have sons and daughters; find wives for your sons and give your daughters in marriage, so that they too may have sons and daughters. Increase in number there; do not decrease. Also, seek the peace and prosperity of the city to which I have carried you into exile. Pray to the Lord for it, because if it prospers, you too will prosper.[4]**

The oppressed Israelites are not to flee the place where they have been exiled; they are to "seek the peace and prosperity" of the city in which God has placed them.

As followers of Jesus, we are called to be the light in the darkness. We do not run from culture; we engage culture with the radical hope of Jesus.

The longing to go back in time to "Kansas" is not helpful, and the desire to physically move to "Kansas" for our comfortability may not be very biblical.

So, are the politics driving many Christians to dream of going back to "the way things were before" irrelevant? No. Far from it.

Christians are to love God and love our neighbor, and the policies we put forward *should* reflect these ideologies.

But while the politics in our community are not irrelevant to Christianity, they aren't our hill to die on, either.

IMPOSING CHRISTIAN ETHICS

What would happen if a profoundly atheistic society were forced to implement Christian values?

I seriously want to consider for a second, what would the result of all this be? What would happen if we told teachers they couldn't talk about Critical Race Theory? What would happen if students weren't allowed to identify as part of the LGBTQ community? What would happen if atheist politicians and teachers were forced to hold corporate prayer gatherings? Would anti-LGBTQ policies cause people to fall in love with Jesus?

Would the removal of Critical Race Theory result in people giving their lives to Jesus? Would mandatory corporate prayer gatherings cause atheists to repent and turn to God? I could be wrong, but something in me just doesn't think this will result in radical heart transformation.

To be sure, I am not advocating that we promote Critical Race Theory or encourage kids to choose their sexuality. I don't think either of these options is helpful. I am also not advocating that prayer doesn't belong in schools. (As a side note, it should be mentioned that students can and *still do* pray in schools. The law has to do with mandatory corporate prayers that are "disruptive" to others.) My point here is not that Christians shouldn't care about these issues or that these issues don't matter. My point is that it will not be these things that bring revival to our country.

Attempting to revert to American Christendom through politics shouldn't be our first priority. Imposing Christian values on
non-Christians rarely results in repentance and the transformation of hearts.

Concerning Christian sexual ethics in the public sector, a 2017
article from the Gospel Coalition writes,

> **The Great Commission is not 'impose Christian
> sexual morality on unbelievers. The progress
> of the Gospel is never by coercion, but by
> preaching, attended with persuasion, suffering,
> and lives of compelling goodness and beauty.
> Any thought that the force of the state could
> advance the Gospel in any way that really
> matters to us should be banished immediately
> to the Really. Bad. Ideas. Folder.**[5]

It's funny. We wouldn't ask our non-Christian friends to follow
our same Christian lifestyle. I have a good friend who is wrestling
with following Jesus. He hasn't given his life over to Christ but is
certainly interested. Like many non-Christians, he has a girlfriend
who he lives with. We have talked about how followers of Jesus
believe that sex is reserved for the covenant of marriage and
why we believe this is God's design for relationships. However, it
wouldn't make sense for me to expect him to give up this life with
his girlfriend unless he professed faith in Jesus. If I spent all my
time trying to get my friend to stop sleeping with his girlfriend,
would this tactic eventually lead him to faith in Jesus? Of course,
the change of heart(s) is what we are after. The lifestyle change
will follow.

The Gospel of Mark outlines the centrality of the heart.

> **For from within, out of the heart of man, come evil thoughts, sexual immorality, theft, murder, adultery, coveting, wickedness, deceit, sensuality, envy, slander, pride, foolishness. All these evil things come from within, and they defile a person.**[6]

When the heart is transformed with the presence of the Holy Spirit, an individual begins to be sanctified through Christ, resulting in a different lifestyle and the putting away of sin.

As the Apostle Paul profoundly states,

> **Therefore, if anyone is in Christ, he is a new creation. The old has passed away; behold, the new has come.**[7]

He is a new creation not because he has put off sin but because he has first put *on* Christ.

Attempting to confront the lifestyle of a non-believer without first approaching the heart is like trimming the top of a weed without first tackling the root; the core issue remains intact even though the outside may appear to be different.

The conversations surrounding CRT, the LGBTQ community, and prayer in schools certainly matter. But they will not be the conversations that lead the next generation to Christ.

Not only is evangelism by politics contrary to the ways of Jesus, but it damages the witness of the church, especially for young people.

JESUS + POLITICS

Recently, I caught up with an old friend over a cup of coffee. We hadn't talked in over five years, and the last time we spoke, he told me he no longer considered himself a Christian. But this time, he shared that he had actually returned to Christianity, even though he still wasn't attending church. Later during our conversation, Covid came up (when does it not in our pandemic age?)

My friend sighed and said, "Man, the churches' response to all of this just makes me sad." "What do you mean?" I asked. I think I knew what he was getting at, but I wanted to hear it from yet another member of Gen Z who has walked away from the church.

"I just feel like this is the reason the church is losing all credibility with young people."

I was a little confused on how he came to this opinion since he isn't attending church.

"Oh, I see it all over social media. For whatever reason, it seems like Christians are the least loving when it comes to Covid stuff. But when I look at the Bible, Jesus seems to be the most loving of all people."

For my friend, it seems that the church cares more about political affiliations and getting people to agree with them than it does about the mission of the church.

Whether you sympathize with my friend's assertion or not, his comments represent the beliefs of many young people I've talked with.

The unfortunate reality is, many young people are leaving the church due to the over-politicizing of Christianity. In many ways, Jesus has become some political symbol instead of our God.

Christian rapper KB reflected:

> I've watched a surge of people I love walk away from Jesus in the last few years… Just about ZERO have been lured away by Marxism, liberalism, or atheism. Almost all have "shipwrecked" over the politicizing of Christianity…[8]

For whatever reason, we have made political ideologies a critical factor in our churches. But this isn't a new problem.

Way back in 1835, Alexis de Tocqueville wrote the first volume of *Democracy in America*, where he foresaw the results of an overly-politicized religion.[9]

Religion does not need [political powers'] assistance to live, and in serving them it can die.

Relying on the power of politics to drive faith forward is a recipe for disaster. But partisanship continues to play a role in what church people attend.

Senior Pastor Dean Inserra, author of *The Unsaved Christian: Reaching Cultural Christianity with the Gospel* says,

> Relocating an influential leader's Sunday School classroom, changing the color of the carpet, going "contemporary" with the music, an unresolved interpersonal conflict, being against the capital campaign. These scenarios used to be the reasons an individual or family would leave a church. While I'm certain those reasons still exist, the new reason people are leaving churches today is American politics.[10]

And for many people, it's not "If the church doesn't agree with my politics, I'm leaving." It's more about churches making political ideologies a primary issue that surpasses following Jesus.

Pastor and Author Carey Nieuwhof explains that post-2020, the political and ideological churches will lose influence with the unchurched.

> Moving ahead a few years, the future church will consist of Christians who look, live, and sound much more like Jesus than the political candidate of their choice.[11]

While politics aren't the main contributor to Gen Z leaving the church, it is distracting us from placing our focus on what matters most.

If we want to see Gen Z fall in love with Jesus, we must be about the things that Jesus is about. We must ruthlessly kill our idols that communicate that the church is more about _____ than the mission of Christ.

The Lordship of Jesus surpasses the realm of space and time. As culture changes, Christ remains the same. He is our only hope. And we must proclaim HIM as our hope; not politics, not cultural relevancy, not woke-ism, and not tribalism.

As Stanley Hauerwas wrote in his classic work *Resident Aliens,*

> The gradual decline of the notion that the church needs some sort of surrounding "Christian" culture to prop it up and mold its young, is not a death to lament. It is an opportunity to celebrate... (This) means that we American Christians are at last free to be faithful in a way that makes being Christian today an exciting adventure.[12]

We're not in Kansas anymore. But that's ok. Because now, following Jesus isn't a cultural norm, but a countercultural reality.

This is the future of the church. One that doesn't know America as *home* yet exists as the radical embodiment of our *true home* in Christ. The sooner we accept that we are no longer in Kansas, the closer we get to representing the counter-cultural Kingdom of Christ to a new generation.

At the intersection of church and culture stands a God who will not be consumed by culture, nor will He hide from it. We must seek to do the same.

The church is not dying.

The church in America is in transition. But transition is not the same as dying.[13] In order to talk about this significant transition, *the church* is exactly where we need to start.

REASONS FOR LEAVING:

- Church is perceived as a political weapon or cultural identity marker instead of Good News that offers hope and life.

- The church is making disciples for Kansas when it needs to be making disciples for a culture that no longer recognizes Jesus as King.

STEPS FOR REACHING Z:

- Keep Jesus the main thing. Instead of longing for the good old days of Christian America, look toward the hope of what God might be doing in the future.

- Teach young people how to be faithful in a culture where Christianity is not widely respected. Encourage students to examine *why* they believe what they believe so they can be resilient disciples of Jesus.

CHAPTER 5

THE CONVERSATION STARTS WITH US

When someone tells me about the vast number of students who leave the church, the comment is usually followed by a brief hypothesis as to why this number is so high. I typically hear something like the following:

> "70 percent of high schoolers will leave the church after they graduate...."

AND

> "What do you expect with the way our culture is going?"

Or

> "It's because of the agenda that colleges are pushing these days."

Or

"Kids today just don't care about God!"

Maybe you have heard something similar to this.

Occasionally, I will hear someone say something like, "I wonder where we as the church are failing to equip our students for a lifelong relationship with Jesus."

However, this response is the exception, not the norm.

More often, the cause of young people leaving the church is believed to be anything BUT *the church*.

Instead, secularism has been adopted as the scapegoat for the church's retention problem.

Once again, as a youth pastor, I would say that our growing secular culture *does* play a part in the greater problem. However, sociologists have observed that secularism is a problem for *all* institutions, not just churches.

In his book *The Great Degeneration*, Niall Ferguson recognizes that the institutions of the West are declining.[1]

> **Alongside the self-interest that has become rampant within private lives within the West, self-interest has become endemic within institutions. This decay has resulted in a growing cynicism as public trust in key institutions fades and, in some cases, disappears altogether.[2]**

In other words, institutions have become less popular because of the rise of individualism and the mistrust of large organizations.

As Author Ray Ortlund puts bluntly, "To call anything an 'institution' today can be its death sentence, including a church."[3]

Secularization has played a key role in the decreased attendance in institutions—including the church.

But we cannot start here.

As long as we continue to blame secular culture for the departure of young people from church, we can be sure to see this number hold steady. While the church can certainly speak to the wider culture, we shouldn't hold our breath waiting for culture to take its cues from the church. Instead, we must focus on what we can change.

As Carl Truemann wrote in his excellent book, *The Rise and Triumph of the Modern Self*,

> **Every age has had its darkness and its dangers. The task of the Christian is not to whine about the moment in which he or she lives but to understand its problems and respond appropriately to them.**[4]

So we can either whine about the current state of Christianity, or we can seek to do something about it.

What's the common denominator in the phrase "70% of church-going students will leave the church when they graduate?" *The church.*

While our growing secular culture plays a role here, students are leaving the church—our people.

> **Our programs.**
> **Our sermons.**
> **Our ministries.**
> **Our community.**

One of the most dangerous things we can do as the church is look at the problem and conclude the blame doesn't reside with us.

WHO'S TO BLAME?

This is probably the wrong question—"Who's to blame?" But it is one that we often ask when it comes to wondering why young people are leaving the church. A better question would be, "Where do we start?" And like any human being that has walked the face of the Earth, we point the finger at anyone *but* ourselves.

When speaking on judgment, Jesus asks a question that should sting all of us a bit:

> **Why do you look at the speck of sawdust in your**
> **brother's eye and pay no attention to the plank**
> **in your own eye?[5]**

It's much easier to point to our brother's flaws than our own. And it's much easier to think the exodus of young people from the church is the fault of Gen Z and society as a whole rather than a fault of our own.

Is Gen Z "at fault" for leaving the church? Sure. There will always be young people who leave the church for reasons that are out of the control of church leadership.

And we could spend time talking about "what's wrong" with this generation of young people. Or I could spend the rest of this book discussing what's wrong with our culture, secularism, and post-modernism. And there have been plenty of good books on that subject.[6]

That said, what I found in my research suggests that if we want to see young people fall in love with Jesus and faithfully participate in the local church, it will do little good to critique what is *outside* the church. If we are waiting for public schools to start preaching sermons in the classroom or for the rest of the world to adopt a biblical model of sexuality and marriage, we may be waiting a while. (And even if these things *did* happen, I'm not so sure it would result in a revival for our youth).

An internal examination of the church is a practice that we see Jesus model.

Jesus could have spent His time on Earth calling out the Gentiles for their foolish and sinful lifestyles. He could have rebuked the Greeks for their belief and practice of mythology. Jesus could have critiqued the growing secular institution of the Roman government, but He didn't. While Jesus certainly had disdain for the heart posture and lifestyles that these people groups and institutions carried forth,[7] He saved His harshest critiques for the religious.

Consider Jesus' confrontation at the temple in John 2:

> In the temple courts He found people selling cattle, sheep and doves, and others sitting at tables exchanging money. So He made a whip out of cords, and drove all from the temple courts, both sheep and cattle; He scattered the coins of the money-changers and overturned their tables.[8]

While we should not use this text to incite violence (note, Jesus never struck anyone or hurt anyone), it *does* contain the most potent example of Jesus' anger toward any person or group of people in all of the Gospels. And, interestingly, this anger is targeted toward the *religious*.

The center of Judaism for those who wanted to worship Yahweh was the temple. It was a place of prayer for them; a geographic location of comfort. More specifically, the *outer courts* were designated for non-Jews. For Gentiles who weren't included in the covenant promise, the outer courts were the only place they could go in the temple. But the Jews had turned this location into a space of buying and selling. The one site that could allow the Gentiles to be included in the Abrahamic covenant had been desecrated.

As one commentator put it,

The promise God made to Abraham, that he would be the father of many nations through Abraham's seed (Jesus)—not just the nation of Israel—was being snuffed out by money-hungry bigots![9]

And Jesus' follow-up words at the temple are strong. Consider the account from Mark's Gospel:

Is it not written: My house will be called a house of prayer for all nations? But you have made it "a den of robbers."[10]

Jesus is quoting the prophet, Isaiah. And according to Isaiah's vision, eunuchs would keep God's covenant,[11] and foreigners would join themselves with Him,[12] and the outcasts would be gathered with His people.[13] But Jesus approached a temple that focused on commerce instead of Isaiah's design. The court of the Gentiles—the place *specifically* designed for foreigners to assemble and for the nations to seek the Lord—was overrun with businesspeople trying to make some money.

And the Jewish leaders had let this happen.[14]

Here's the key: For. All. Nations.

Not just the Jewish elites.

Jesus' comment is *even more* of an insult to the Jews because He quotes one of *their own* prophets, Isaiah. The Jews would have known these words well, which places them under further scrutiny.

Why? Because they *should* know.

The Jews knew the Torah. It would make sense if the Gentiles were the ones instigating the all-out garage sale in the temple. But the Jews should have known better.

This is where I want to sit for a second.

The church. The followers of Jesus. The ones who know the Word of God. WE should know better.

We should know better than to blame the problem of the 70% on outside sources and institutions.

And while we should call our young people to a higher standard of Christian living, we shouldn't use them as our scapegoats either.

We are responsible.

I don't want to draw a one-to-one connection to the 1st century temple and the American church in the 21st century, Jesus' words should echo loud and clear for us today.

The ones who bear responsibility for faith inside the church are not the Gentiles but the religious. And faith leaders will be judged more harshly because of their place of calling and leadership.[15]

In the Gospels, it is always the religious who Jesus seems to take issue with; and we should ask if Jesus would also take issue with us today.

What practices would Jesus drive out from our local church?

What are the ways that we have made it difficult for others—the outsider, the non-religious, the skeptic, the doubter, *Gen Z*, to be part of our church?

Have we turned our churches into institutions that have made the main thing—proclaiming the name of Jesus and fostering a Christlike community—into a secondary thing?

When we ask, "Why do 70% of high schoolers leave the church when they graduate?", we have to start with the church.

As much as Jesus' remarks were a condemnation, condemnation was not the goal.

For Jesus, critiquing the religious elite was less about bringing about shame and guilt and more about ushering in a new way of life. It was about transforming the human heart.

His motivation wasn't just for us to be sorry, but for us to be changed. To more truly resemble our Creator in thought, word, and deed.

So, when we think about the 70% of young people leaving the church, let us consider Jesus' call; that His House would resemble the words of the prophets. And that the church would bring about life change, not just in the hearts of those who don't know Him, but in the hearts of those who are shepherding His church.

As you read this book, I encourage you to do a thorough examination of your church, your ministry, and your heart. If we want to see God launch a revival in our country, we must get out of the way.

If we desire to see Generation Z come to know Jesus and we want God to use *us* as part of His redemptive plan, we must set aside our presuppositions and objectively examine our heart and our ministry. Once we do this, God can begin to work change in our hearts and shift our narratives to start telling the story He wants us to tell.

So, when we ask, "Why have so many young people left the church?", a faithful, humble response would be, "There are many reasons. But the conversation starts with us."

TEARING DOWN AND BUILDING UP

A movement that has been picking up steam, especially with young people, is deconstruction. Simply put, deconstruction is a term that refers to the practice of revisiting or rethinking long-held beliefs and practices, specifically in the Christian faith. Some have championed a faith process that takes place in three stages:

- **Construction** – building your belief system and worldview

- **Deconstruction** – challenging that worldview and subsequent beliefs

- **Reconstruction** – rebuilding a new, more holistic set of beliefs and worldview[16]

Of course, deconstruction is one of those loaded terms that means different things to different people. Some take deconstruction to mean abandoning the faith completely, while others take it to mean simply rethinking faith.

Re-thinking the foundation and truthfulness of one's beliefs can be an incredibly healthy practice for people of faith because it prompts us to consider *why* we believe what we believe.

The Bible commands us to scrutinize our faith, making sure what we believe is actually of God and Scripture.[17] This process also promotes personal inspection of one's faith journey, recalling certain key events and faith practices. Sometimes, deconstruction reveals the pain that has been caused by well-intentioned but misled Christians.

At its best, deconstruction is prophetic.

It highlights the ways in which the people of God have failed to live according to truth and love and encourages them toward the ways of Jesus.

But at its worst, deconstruction is demolition.

Here, there is every intention of tearing down the church and God's people without the purpose of building them up.

And to be sure, the church *often needs* a punch to the gut (the Israelites took quite a few of these punches from the prophets). The prophets were actually concerned with the state of the Israelites and their faith in Yahweh. But the danger of the rise of Christian "deconstruction" is that it neither loves nor rebuilds. As followers of Jesus, we should always desire the church to embody Christ in thought, word, and deed. We should long for all Christians to love God with all their heart, soul, mind, and strength and to love their neighbor as themselves.

Critique is often necessary when we fail to live up to the high calling of God's people. Deconstruction is important. But it is important for the purpose of *building back up.*

In our examination of why Generation Z is leaving the church, I am not seeking to provide a laundry list of reasons why the church is terrible and why things are rather hopeless. This will not be an account of Christian deconstruction.

Sure, there are *many* things within the church that need refinement. We certainly need to better understand and relate to the next generation. But the intention of this critique is that the church would more clearly live out its mission to be the hope of the world in a culture that no longer recognizes Jesus as King.

Sometimes we forget, the church was *GOD'S* idea. Not ours. So the church isn't going anywhere. We aren't going to deconstruct it until it collapses. That's not possible. The church is the hope of the world, and God does not *need us* to "fix" it. But how cool is it that He asks us to partner with Him? Therefore, in this partnership, let's seek to be good stewards, hardworking teammates, that we may see God's Kingdom come, and His will be done on Earth as it is in Heaven.

REASONS FOR LEAVING:

- The church often looks outside itself to address the problem of young people leaving.

STEPS FOR REACHING Z:

- Accept ownership for Gen Z leaving the church. While secular culture plays a role in this problem, let's focus on what we can control as the church.

PART 2

REACHING
GEN Z

CHAPTER 6

LITTLE RASCALS AND HORROR MOVIES

In order to think about engaging Generation Z with the hope of Jesus, we must first consider the story we have been telling about our young people and the narrative that underlines our beliefs and practices.

There is a narrative about young people today that clouds our judgment, limits the value of youth, and inhibits the Kingdom potential of the church.

Many of us see young people as "Little Rascals" who stir up trouble in our church and communities. The old saying "Kids these days" rings true for how many church leaders think about Gen Z.

While the perception of youth as "Little Rascals" is often conveyed through humor, it's the small comments and decisions by leaders that illustrate to Gen Z just how unimportant they are in the eyes of the church. This attitude understands young people to be *projects* instead of *partners* in the Gospel. They are seen not as people to be loved but people to be fixed.

A common stereotype of young people can be summed up in one word: millennial. You know what I mean. "Millennial' can be used almost interchangeably with words like lazy, entitled, and selfish.

Check out one of the Urban Dictionary definitions of millennial: "The name an old person gives a young person they don't like."[1] That's rough.

Of course, the technical definition of a millennial is someone born between 1980-1995. The young people we see in our churches now are no longer millennials, but the apathetic stigma still remains.

When we think about the future of the church—the women and men who will be leading our churches—we have to start with Generation Z. And we cannot expect to have wise, humble, holy, and faithful leaders if we continue with such a pessimistic attitude toward young people.

When we talk about why Generation Z is leaving the church, we must consider our negative stereotypes of young people. If we don't confront this issue, it will continue to be an obstacle in the way of leading Gen Z to a vibrant faith in Jesus.

FEAR

The first horror movie I ever watched was *Paranormal Activity*. In high school, a few of my friends and I got together on a Saturday night and amped ourselves up to watch. The movie was basically about a couple who moves into a new house and discovers that the house is haunted. Classic, I know. But the crazy part of the movie is that somebody recorded it through a personal camera. It looked like someone was filming a live-action shot of what was taking place in this creepy house. And this movie haunted me for weeks. Whenever I was at home alone, I had to keep the lights on all the time and make sure the doors and windows were locked.

I want to propose that the American church has allowed the narrative of fear to drive its thoughts, words, and actions. We may not overtly announce, "I'm scared," but we make sure all the hypothetical doors and windows are locked. We especially find this attitude in the way we talk about and act towards our non-Christian neighbors.

The narrative of fear has driven many of us to go into all-out protection mode, fearing the outside world and deeming all things non-Christian as evil.

The theme of fear is one that comes up time and time again in the life of the church. And it is a theme that causes young people to consider whether or not they want to continue being part of a community that uses this principle to underline many of its beliefs and practices.

In the book, *You Lost Me—Why Young Christians are Leaving the Church, and Rethinking Faith,* David Kinnaman, and the Barna

Research Group conducted eight national studies, including interviews with teenagers, young adults, parents, youth pastors, and senior pastors. The study of young adults focused on regular churchgoers during their teen years and explored the reasons for their disconnection from church life after age 15. I should note that this book was released in 2011; however, the research should give us a good idea of where many teens stand today.[2]

In this study, Kinnaman gives six primary reasons young people leave the church. One of the reasons they give is:

"Churches seem overprotective."

Barna found that:

> **A few of the defining characteristics of today's teens and young adults are their unprecedented access to ideas and worldviews as well as their prodigious consumption of popular culture. As Christians, they express the desire for their faith in Christ to connect to the world they live in. However, much of their experience of Christianity feels stifling, fear-based and risk-averse.[3]**

While the church *should* offer a different way of living than the surrounding secular culture, the issue is when fear is utilized to scare our young people *away* from the secular culture. We perceive culture as a significant threat to spiritual life, so we demonize all things non-Christian.

A way that would better resemble Scripture and the life of Jesus would be to promote Christ as the better alternative. Instead of demonizing culture, we are to magnify Christ.

In another one of his studies titled *unchristian*, Kinnaman notes,

> **We (the church) have become more famous for what we oppose instead of what we are for.**[4]

And we have earned this reputation in part because we spend significant time and energy speaking on what we are *against* instead of the Jesus we are *for.*

According to Kinnaman, students feel this overprotective mentality from the church, which causes them to rethink participating in the church community.

But this overprotective mentality is the result of a deeper problem, which goes back to the perception of "Little Rascals."

In Barna's *The State of Youth Ministry*, Sharon Galgay Ketcham articulates this fear mentality concerning our youth.

> **There is a well-known narrative shaping our perception of teenagers. The narrative is as old as the socially created category "teenager" that emerged in the 1900s. We hear it daily in the media, in helicopter parenting and even in our approaches to youth ministry: the idea that teenagers are broken, deficient, and in need of help. We problematize teenagers and use**

significant resources to try and fix them. This narrative evokes fear...[5]

The story goes something like this: *If we don't protect teenagers from the evils of this world, then who will?* Of course, this ideology forces God out of the equation.

In the process of trying to protect and fix our young people, we subtly play the role of God in the redeeming process. No longer is it the work of the Holy Spirit to renew and sanctify our teenagers; it is *our* work, which is often driven by a scarcity or overprotective mindset.

This communicates the image of a rather small God and a big and dangerous world. And of course, there *are* real dangers in our world. The question is, how do we care for our children in light of these dangers?

While some of this protective attitude derives from healthy skepticism, some derives from unhealthy fear. When I read Jesus and Paul's letters, "safe living" does not seem to be one of the main themes.

Dying to self, weakness, and suffering *are* central themes displayed by Christ and the early church.[6]

Paul went as far as to say,

> Therefore, I delight in weaknesses, in insults, in distresses, in persecutions, in difficulties, in behalf of Christ; for when I am weak, then I am strong.[7]

It isn't power, control, and safety that leads to strength, but weakness.

Jesus saw the urgency and importance of His mission. He didn't let the prospect of dangerous people or non-Jewish communities pull Him off His mission.

The outsiders were His *mission*.

But they have become our *threat*.

The people Jesus crossed boundaries for are the same people we put up walls against.

And if we don't give our young people any opportunities to be creative, experience new things, to try and fail, then perhaps we are not preparing them for a life lived for Jesus. Furthermore, we are not preparing them for life after high school.

In a practical sense, we understand that the more experiences and exposure young people have to different perspectives (even non-Christian perspectives), the more apt they are to respond thoughtfully and holistically to various situations.[8] When students are exposed to a single ideology and raised in an echo chamber of sorts, they witness activities, voices, and perspectives that shock their system after high school.

This culture shock can result in young people questioning their upbringing and rethinking their faith. But when students are exposed to these same things at a younger age and within the context of Christian discipleship, then they can struggle alongside wise adults in a safe environment.

Spreading the narrative of fear communicates to young people that God's sovereignty is in question. After all, how powerful is the God we serve if we are taught to constantly "watch out for this" and "avoid that?"

For many, American Christianity has become more about a list of don'ts and less about being on a mission for Jesus. Choosing to follow Jesus is seen as some sort of delayed gratification where I don't get to do a bunch of fun stuff here on Earth, but I'll get the payout when I get to Heaven one day. It has become passive avoidance instead of missional engagement. We see this play out in family dynamics as well.

PARENTING

There are really two camps when it comes to research on parenting techniques, and Generation Z. One camp is the "helicopter camp," which believes most Gen Xers are overprotective of their Gen Z children. The other camp believes that most Gen X parents are under-protective, partly in an attempt to avoid the helicopter label.[9] So the research is a bit conflicted.

Barna offers that perhaps reality lies somewhere in the middle. Parents are overprotective in some ways and under-protective in others. This is likely the case.

Speaking against the overprotective position, journalist Hannah Rosin argues:

> **A preoccupation with safety has stripped childhood of independence, risk taking, and discovery, without making it safer. In 1971, 80%**

of third-graders walked to school alone. By 1990, that measure had dropped to 9%, and now it's even lower.[10]

Barna responds, "The problem is, the world is not more dangerous; we just perceive it that way."

According to an article from the *New York Times,* America's violent crime rate is about half of what it was in 1991.[11]

Polling shows that Americans persistently believe crime is worse than it actually is. And according to research by Barna Group for Prison Fellowship, evangelicals are "far more likely than the general American public" to make this mistake.[12]

The result from overprotecting our kids, Rosin concludes, is devastating:

> A continuous and ultimately dramatic decline in children's opportunities to play and explore in their own chosen ways. Finally, children have become less emotionally expressive, less energetic, less talkative and verbally expressive, less humorous, less imaginative, less unconventional, less lively and passionate, less perceptive, less apt to connect seemingly irrelevant things, less synthesizing, and less likely to see things from a different angle.[13]

This is just sad.

The impact of fear-based parenting has lasting effects on the lives of young people. In her book *How to Raise an Adult,* Julie Lythcott-Haims, explains,

> **Kids with over-involved parents and rigidly structured childhoods suffer psychological blowback in college. While protecting kids in their youth may make them "safe," this lifestyle of safe living doesn't always correlate into their next stages of life.**[14]

Social scientist and professor Jean Twenge explains the impact of protective parenting and the result this has on teen formation. In her findings, Twenge notes that teens go out less, wait longer to have sex, and drink less alcohol. Furthermore, teen pregnancies have plummeted.[15] (Am I the only person who is SHOCKED by this data?)

This is all good news, right?

Well, not entirely.

The "binge" lifestyle sets in when students graduate high school and enter college. While teens live low-risk in their high school years, they are setting records for the prevalence of alcohol, drugs, and sexual activity in their college years. In essence, they are just putting off these behaviors until college, only to indulge more frequently and in greater quantities than they would in high school.[16]

So, what does this mean? That we just allow our kids to experiment with drugs and alcohol in high school? Absolutely not.

But there is a correlation between over-protecting teens and delayed rebellion after high school. In addition to this, what does it communicate about the power of our God if we are constantly worried about the influence of the outside world? Are we telling our young people that God really *is* in control?

THE SAFE LION

In C. S. Lewis's novel *The Lion, the Witch, and the Wardrobe*, of *The Chronicles of Narnia*, Susan asks Mr. Beaver what Aslan (who symbolizes God) is really like.

When she discovers that Aslan is a lion, Susan remarks,

> "Ooh!" said Susan, "I'd thought he was a man. Is he—quite safe? I shall feel rather nervous about meeting a lion." "Safe?" said Mr. Beaver. "Who said anything about safe? 'Course he isn't safe. But he's good. He's the King, I tell you."[17]

As C.S. Lewis beautifully illustrates, Jesus is anything but safe.

In Matthew 10, Jesus tells His disciples, "You will be hated by everyone because of me."[18]

And in the Gospel of John, Jesus warns, "A servant is not greater than his master. If they persecuted me, they will persecute you."[19]

Author Shane Claiborne says it like this:

> So if the world hates us, we take courage that it hated Jesus first. If you're wondering whether

you'll be safe, just look at what they did to Jesus and those who followed Him. There are safer ways to live than by being a Christian.[20]

Sometimes I wonder if we are training our teens to believe that Christianity is safe, the world is evil, and we should avoid people who are part of the latter. I wonder if we are taming the Gospel and the life of Jesus into cute stories and moral lessons. Sometimes we forget that Jesus was a single, homeless Jew who washed feet and hung out with prostitutes and tax collectors.

In many ways, we have domesticated Jesus and therefore domesticated our Christianity. No wonder young people are leaving the church. There is an incongruence between the radical Jesus and the institution of the church. One embraces danger, and the other leverages fear to keep it out.

I remember when I got a call from a parent who was concerned about the state of our youth ministry. He shared that he was worried about "all the gay kids" coming to the youth group. I thought he would ask about our theology of sexuality or our sermons, but this was not what he was getting at.

I'll never forget when he said, "Church used to be a safe place where I could drop my kids off."

This was the crux of the issue for him. Certain people made church unsafe.

And don't get me wrong. We should be fostering a community where parents feel safe dropping off their kids.

But if we are creating a theology around safe living—where certain groups of people are marked as dangerous—then I'm afraid we won't have much Scripture to back it up.

Many of us would rather have a safe church than a church that includes the people Jesus was concerned about. We forget that Christians around the world face real persecution that may cost them their lives, while we are concerned about that which will cost us our comfort.

Instead of teaching that following Jesus means avoiding culture, behaviors, and people who don't think or look like us, what if we dared students to participate in the mission of Jesus?

If we start to change the way we think *about* young people, we will begin to see a change *in* our young people.

When we believe young people are not just problems to be fixed, but rather the future of the church, we can begin to empower Gen Z to lead as Christ intended.

And if we begin to challenge our students to participate in God's Kingdom mission here on Earth, not just to tiptoe through life safely, then perhaps we will see young people embody the bold faith of Jesus.

REASONS FOR LEAVING:

- Young people are perceived as "Little Rascals" who need to be fixed. As a result, young people feel looked down on and unimportant. This limits their Kingdom potential as Christ-followers.

- The church is perceived as "overprotective," which communicates to Gen Z there is a big, dangerous world and a small, risk-averse God.

STEPS FOR REACHING Z:

- Start believing the best about young people and empowering them in your church. Gen Z are the leaders of tomorrow *as well as* leaders of *today.*

- Challenge young people with the most incredible mission of all time. Following Jesus won't be safe or easy, but WOW will it be worth it.

CHAPTER 7

SYSTEM
STUDENTS

"He's a system guy."

If you've been around competitive sports, you've probably heard this phrase. When people say she or he is a "system guy," they are usually stating that the player is good because they are part of a good team or system. In other words, it's the coach that makes them great, or it's the schematics and play calling that makes them successful. But really, when you take them out of the system, they fall apart. Because the system was set up for them to have the most success in one specific area, they usually lacked competency in other areas.

A great example of this is the Christian favorite and all-around American hero (I'm only slightly kidding), Tim Tebow.

Tim Tebow is widely regarded as one of the greatest college football players of all time. Fox Sports recently rated him as the #10 greatest college football player ever. He was the first player ever to record 20 rushing touchdowns and 20 passing touchdowns in one season. He led Florida to two national titles and became the first sophomore ever to win the Heisman when he threw for 3,286 yards and rushed for 895 yards with 55 total touchdowns in 2007.[1]

However, he started just 16 total games and only lasted three years in the NFL. He recently attempted to make a comeback with the Jaguars in 2021, but was cut almost immediately. How could someone be so good in college, yet flop in the NFL?

He was a system guy.

Tebow excelled in college because the University of Florida created an offensive system that catered to his skill set and ability. This system gave Tebow opportunities to run the football as well as throw for medium and short gains through the air—things that he was gifted in. But at the NFL level, he wasn't fast enough to run the football with success and wasn't strong enough to make the long and accurate throws down the field.

He excelled in college because he fit the system well. But this didn't translate into the NFL.

I believe one of the reasons we see many young people leaving the church is because we set them up to be great youth group attenders, not great followers of Jesus.

We are obsessed with creating the best youth ministry system, but once a student graduates from this system, they don't know how to live out their faith in the context of the larger church community.

Of course, this completely depends on your "system."

I've seen plenty of young people who didn't attend youth group in high school and didn't seem to have a strong relationship with Jesus, but when they graduated all of this changed. They became faithful members of the church community and grew exponentially in their walk with Christ. This could be for a variety of different reasons.

Or maybe your team has sat down and talked through how you can create a youth ministry that is attractive to young people, but still equips, trains, and disciples them for life after youth ministry.

But if you are anything like me, you have been swallowed up in the corporate machine that is youth ministry.

Not only are youth pastors responsible for leading students to faith in Jesus in their teens, but they are also responsible for making this faith stick in their 20s and 30s.

It's difficult to partner with other ministry leaders in various areas of the church to think about how a young person will live out their faith in their 20s when you are constantly thinking through the next event, the next camp, or the next mission trip. I get it. And this may be part of the issue in and of itself.

Part of the responsibility of a youth pastor is understanding that the discipleship of each student is *not* solely your responsibility. A saying we communicate often at our church is "We believe parents are the primary disciple-makers of their own kids." In other words, teaching children how to follow Jesus is first and foremost the responsibility of the child's parents.

As a youth ministry, we never want to operate like a dry cleaner: Drop your kid off at youth group and the ministry returns them all neat and clean, equipped with a biblical worldview. Why doesn't this work? Well for one, Scripture seems to outline a clear role for parents to train up their children. Deuteronomy 6 and Ephesians 6 indicate this in detail. So as a youth ministry, we don't want parents to abdicate their God-given responsibility to teach their children the ways of Jesus.

Second, the youth ministry as a "one-stop-shop" for discipleship doesn't work because discipleship cannot occur (at least not effectively) in a vacuum.

When we look at the way Jesus did discipleship—and even the early church—it was life-on-life teaching involving experiences and hands-on training. A youth ministry may get 2-3 hours a week with students, while parents have infinitely more interactions with their kids.

Part of the problem of the "system" of youth ministry is the belief that the youth ministry *is* the end all be all when it comes to discipling young people. But if we want to see students engaged with the Gospel in a holistic manner, we have to make parents a priority in our ministry.

We can either be passive or active in engaging parents with discipling their students. A passive response is simply recognizing that the parents should be pulling some weight, but not doing anything about it. This response assumes the parents *are* actively discipling their kids, but it doesn't take any steps towards supporting, equipping, or encouraging those parents.

An active role recognizes the biblical responsibility parents have to train their kids in the ways of Jesus *and* seeks to establish a "teamwork" mindset in discipling those students. Here, the youth ministry isn't an "instead-of" but an "in-addition-to" family discipleship.

"What if a student doesn't have Christian parents to disciple them?"

Yep. That's the question we should always be considering when discipling students. And if this is the case, it's a chance for the church to really be the church in communally guiding this young person in their walk with Christ.

I would say that 30-40% of the students at our youth group do not have parents who attend our church. We still think that parent has a biblical responsibility to disciple their student, but we realize that this discipleship probably isn't happening at home.

One of our students, whose parents are not believers, has been sort of "spiritually adopted" by a family at our church. She spends hours at their home and the parents take the time to have intentional conversations with her concerning faith, school, and just life in general. This won't be the case for every spiritual orphan. For some, the church's youth pastor may play the role of spiritual parent. Or, as our Pastor of Seniors likes to say, some grandparents may adopt "surrogate grandchildren." This is where students who do not have a Christian adult influence can be mentored and discipled by an older person in the church. And this isn't only a benefit for the students, but it empowers adults to take on a discipleship role, as we are ALL called to.[2]

Part of the "system of youth ministry" problem lies in the heart of the mission. If we believe that in order for a student to become a fully devoted follower of Christ, *our* youth ministry must be the driving force, then we're missing the point. If we believe God needs *our* youth ministry to train *His* children, then we've formed a diminished view of God and an enhanced view of ourselves.

We believe God is a relational being. He wants to partner with creation in carrying out His Kingdom work here on Earth. But we need to think about our youth ministry in a holistic manner that engages parents, grandparents, teachers, coaches, and others to disciple our young people—not *just* the youth pastor.

By doing so, we avoid building the narrow system of youth ministry and we begin to equip the saints for ministry as outlined in Ephesians 4.[3] Here, we don't win only when *our ministry* is directly involved in discipling students, we win when the Gospel is proclaimed, with or without us. This is better for the student, better for the church, and better for the Kingdom. Prioritizing parents in youth ministry creates a holistic form of discipleship that *includes* the youth group but is not limited to it.

DISSECTING THE SYSTEM

Think about your youth ministry system. How is your youth group discipling students to be lifelong followers of Jesus, not just youth group all-stars? Part of this examination process includes thinking through the practices within the youth ministry that are more focused on building up the youth group than they are on building disciples.

We should also be asking, "What are the things we're doing in the youth ministry that will not be transferable when students enter 'Big church?'" (I don't like that word but there it is).

Of course, this doesn't mean that youth ministry-specific events and programming should be eliminated from the youth group. Not at all. I think we need to simply take notice that these types of events won't be driving their faith post-high school. In light of this, maybe this means setting up times when youth group doesn't *always* have the traditional crazy youth ministry madness. Maybe sometimes, youth group has other spiritual elements that reflect an environment more like church on Sunday mornings.

But I'm not saying that simply changing the "childish" parts of youth ministry sets up young people for success post-high school. This is far too narrow of a focus.

More importantly, we need to communicate to our young people what it looks like to be a follower of Jesus, period. Yes, this is obvious, but it's not always easy.

Designing our youth ministries to teach young people how to follow Jesus in a holistic manner that incorporates youth group, yes; but also includes church, family, vocation, relationships, and other aspects of life that faith should be incorporated into. This trains young people to think about faith in a way that exists outside of the realm of youth group.

We can teach our young people that youth group is important because it connects our faith to a community of believers (the church) but that following Jesus should infiltrate all areas of our life, not only our youth ministry life.

Dr. Ron Marrs, who was a youth pastor for over 25 years, strategically thought through faith outside of youth group, by incorporating practical classes that would train students on things like vocation and college prep. This taught students to think about how following Jesus would exist in other areas of life, such as the areas of work and education.

Furthermore, this process illustrated to young people that the church isn't just about getting you saved, but it is about training you how to follow Jesus in ways that practically intersect with all areas of your life. It communicates that the church cares about the whole person, not just the individual at church. It shows young people that we *want* you to succeed at being a student, being an employee, and being a member of your family; and we believe that the way of Jesus has something to say about all of these matters, not just the matters of the church.

Thinking about following Jesus in such a holistic way allows young people to participate in the ways of Jesus, not just as youth group attenders, but as faithful disciples.

This ideology does not have to exist only in a programmatic kind of way like a class or a lesson plan. Nor should it.

The idea that being a follower of Jesus should impact all areas of one's life should be the language we use when we preach, when we lead small groups, when we disciple someone one on one, and even when we attend a student's soccer game.

Consider this. Say you are leading a small group of 8th grade girls. You ask them, "What did you get out of the message?" Nothing wrong with this question. Next, you ask, "Did you attend youth group last week?" "If not, why weren't you there?" Ok, this is still important. Following this question, you ask the girls, "How has your relationship with Jesus impacted your relationships with students in youth group?"

There isn't anything inherently wrong with any of these questions. I ask many of them myself. The problem shows up when the *only* conversations you have about faith are related to youth group or the church. What this communicates is that following Jesus boils down to how I exist at the church building, not how I exist as an actual embodiment of the church in the world.

If you are a paid ministry person or a dedicated volunteer, sometimes we can fall into this trap.

Because *our* lives exist in and around the church building, we interact with people as if *their* lives do as well. We don't ask questions about their families or latest vacations. We don't consider how their faith is intersecting with their time at school or work.

Such a narrow perspective of church slowly seeps into comments, questions, and even sermons.

Perhaps, this is why many young people get burned out on church and eventually leave. Our Western American perspective has turned church into a building instead of a people.

Students are taught how to follow Jesus at church, the importance of attending camps and retreats, and why they should volunteer on Sundays. But they rarely see the church coming to them, or the church taking interest in the things of their life.

The Bible certainly outlines a model of church that goes beyond the narrow confines of a building and stretches to the inward parts of the life of the individual. Consider the early church in the book of Acts:

> All the believers were together and had every-thing in common. They sold property and possessions to give to anyone who had need. Every day they continued to meet together in the temple courts. They broke bread in their homes and ate together with glad and sincere hearts.[4]

The model of church we get in the New Testament is one that *is* relevant to the life of the individual; not in a self-centered way, but in a communal way. While the church certainly does not exist for the interests of the individual, it is inherently connected to the individual as the visible representation of the image of God.

So, while we don't want people to be asking about church, "What's in it for me?", we would also say that there certainly *is* something in it for you. It just might not be exactly what you are expecting.

Kara Powell from Fuller Seminary recalls a comment made by a 15-year-old student: "I'm tired of church answering all of the questions I don't care about."

Kara notes that this should be a comment that all church leaders keep in the back of their minds.[5] We always need to be thinking about who we are speaking to and consider what they may be dealing with in their personal life.

When asked why they are leaving the church, many young people give an answer like the following: "I just don't see how church is relevant to my life."

For many students, it isn't that they don't believe in God. And it isn't that they don't know the Gospel intellectually; it's simply that they don't see how the church matters to their life, right now.

We should eliminate language that communicates faith exists exclusively within the confines of a building.

The Greek word for church, "ekklesia" literally means "called out ones." The church was never intended to be referred to as a building, but as the gathered physical embodiment of Christ's hope here on Earth.[6]

One of the dangers of referring to church primarily as a physical location is that it separates the sacred from the secular. Typically,

Christians tend to think of things as Christian or non-Christian. We classify things or events as Christian or secular: Christian music or secular music, Christian parties or secular parties.

We see church on Sunday as Christian, but not the rest of life.

Maybe this is why many people dress differently, talk differently, and sometimes act entirely differently at "church" on Sunday than they do the rest of the week. And maybe living two separate lives (sacred vs. secular) is another factor that contributes to young people feeling burdened, and eventually walking away from church.

Discussing the problem of separating the sacred from the secular, Pastor Jeff Vanderstelt writes,

> **And those who are not yet a part of the church or have left it want nothing to do with it because it doesn't seem to have anything to do with the rest of life. However, the Scriptures don't define church or Christians this way. Neither do they define life this way. It's not activities and events that are primarily Christian. It's people. Activities and events, by themselves, are not sacred, but people are.[7]**

This separation of the sacred from the secular also contributes to the "us vs. them" mentality (which we talked about earlier) that many Christians have toward their non-Christian neighbors.

When we gauge one's spiritual formation primarily by their attendance in church services and events, we are contributing to this sort of separation mindset.

As pastors, we can say "The church is not a building" as much as we want, but until we start living this out in our discipleship philosophy, people won't believe us.

This means being OK with lower numbers *at* programs and classes if we know our people are engaging *as* the church in their communities. If we really believe the church is a gathered body of believers, then church can take place in whatever setting contains this body of believers.

Why is the conversation about the definition of church so important?

Because for whatever reason, some young people have come to believe that they can follow Jesus without the church. But what they often *really* believe is they can follow Jesus without stepping inside a building *called* church.

When we begin talking about church as the gathered body of believers, and when our ministries reflect this language, our young people will begin to understand following Jesus in a holistic sense; a way of life that *includes* a building called church but extends to all of life *as the church*.

We need the physical building called church as a place where followers of Jesus can gather, pray, encourage, learn, lament, forgive, celebrate, and worship, but we also need this same gathered people to leave Sunday afternoon with a sense that they are now going out as the embodiment of Christ's Kingdom here on Earth.

WISDOM IN THE SYSTEM

When we think about the dangers of creating "system students"—students that thrive in a youth ministry setting but fail to adapt to following Jesus post-high school—we should think about *who* we are utilizing to train the students in this system.

Let me put it this way.

If Tim Tebow were surrounded by coaches who came from a variety of different systems, who could train him not just to operate the Florida Gators offense, but NFL offenses as well, would this better prepare him for an NFL career? I think so.

I have had the privilege of serving as a youth pastor at three different churches in three different states. I have seen a variety of youth ministry models and I've come to understand that there certainly isn't a one-size-fits-all model of youth ministry. Different ministries have different missions and visions, and these different ministries function in different cultural contexts.

With this being said, I always wonder about a youth ministry model that only utilizes young adult volunteers. I have seen youth ministries that exclusively recruit leaders who are under 30. I see the value in this. You are using the gifts and abilities of young people who know what it's like to be a middle or high schooler, because they were just in that season of life themselves.

But limiting the volunteer role for student ministries to young adults is like building a team of NFL rookies (Sorry, I need to stop with the football stuff). Sure, you get the passion, energy, and talents of the young people, but you lack some of the wisdom and experience from older people.

If we want our young people to be lifelong followers of Jesus, we need to surround them with younger leaders AND older leaders. If we want to see students stick with their faith past high school and college, we need intergenerational leaders who know what it looks like to follow Jesus consistently past high school or college.

While a twentysomething small group leader is great, a 60-year-old small group leader can provide experiences, wisdom, and perspectives that a twentysomething can't.

Older believers discipling younger believers is modeled throughout Scripture, and this is demonstrated powerfully through the apostle Paul's relationship with Timothy. Timothy accompanied Paul on his journeys and their relationship deepened to the point that Paul called Timothy "my true son in the faith."[8]

Barna Research Institute found that young people who have an adult mentor at their church are *three times more likely* to continue attending church after high school than those who didn't have a mentor.[9]

This is why one of the best things we can do is surround our young people with godly adult mentors.

Consider what seminary professor Chap Clark says:

> **Here's the bottom line: Every kid needs five adult fans. Any young person who shows any interest in Christ needs a minimum of five people of various ages who will say, "I'm going to love that kid until they are fully walking as an adult member of this congregation."**[10]

Chap is talking about getting five people on your team who believe in you and want to support you in your faith journey.

Be on somebody's team. Root for them. Pray for them. Believe in them.

I love this model that Chap Clark offers because it doesn't require a whole lot from an adult. Clark isn't saying that every young person needs five people who will do a weekly Bible study with them. He's simply saying that the student needs to know they have an adult in their corner. This adult is here if they have a question or doubt, or simply to celebrate with the student when they succeed.

Growing up, I wasn't part of a youth group. But I remember being a high school sophomore when Fellowship of Christian Athletes launched a ministry at our school. The leader of FCA, Trevor, asked me if I wanted to grab coffee sometime. From here, Trevor and I met consistently for almost three years until I graduated high school. Trevor opened the Bible with me, taught me how to study Scripture, and showed me what it looked like to pursue Christ in all areas of life.

My freshman year of college was difficult and lonely at times. But you know who drove eight hours to visit me? Trevor.

When I encountered some interesting theology from a church I started attending in college, you know who I called? Trevor.

When I felt God's prompting to go into full-time ministry, you know who affirmed God's calling on my life? Trevor.

When I began writing this book and sought advice, you know who counseled and encouraged me? Yep. Trevor.

For over 10 years, Trevor has believed in me, rooted for me, and discipled me. I know that whenever I'm struggling or need advice, he will be there.

As amazing as Trevor is and for how profoundly he impacted my life, more than anything, he was simply available. It didn't take a seminary degree or a teaching curriculum. Trevor showed up in my life *regularly and consistently*, which completely transformed my faith in Jesus.

If every young person had a Trevor, someone who consistently cared about them and pointed them to Jesus, I think we would start to see a dent in that big 70%.

One particular practice that brings students into meaningful relationships with other generations is a Rite of Passage.

Recently, I was part of a send-off ceremony for one of our graduating seniors. The parents of this senior sat down with him and asked, "Who have been some of the most influential people in your life?" About five men gathered together to say a blessing over this senior and to pray for him as he left for college. While the blessing and prayer are meant to encourage and lift up the student to God, there is another dynamic impact that this event has on the student.

A Rite of Passage communicates that there are godly people in your local church who love you and who are rooting for you. No matter what. This helps the student to connect community, friendship, support, and love to the local church. This leaves the student with a positive perception of church and illustrates just how important it is to be part of a community of believers.

Intergenerational models of ministry help young people think past what faith looks like in high school. Adult influences provide a variety of experiences and perspectives that help students grow in their faith journey.

Creating youth group all-stars, while it may get young people excited about following Jesus, is far too narrow-minded when thinking through how these same students will follow Jesus for a lifetime.

When we create an environment that thinks past the walls of the youth ministry room and the church building, we are closer to creating disciples for a lifetime, not just a time period.

REASONS FOR LEAVING:

- We've created a segment of youth group attendees instead of Christ-followers.

- Students don't have Christlike adult mentors in their life.

STEPS FOR REACHING Z:

- Design a youth ministry that teaches young people how to follow Jesus in a holistic sense. Teach them how to *be* the church, not just how to attend.

- Empower adult leaders from *all* ages. Make sure the older generation knows their important role in discipling the younger generation.

CHAPTER 8

BE REAL, BRO

If you've been around teenagers lately, you know that the worst thing someone could possibly be is fake.

In fact, if there was a single characteristic valued by Generation Z, its authenticity. For a member of Gen Z, not only is being authentic important, but it's actually what makes someone cool.

Data reported by CNBC shows that authenticity is a critical value for Gen Z:

> 67 percent of those surveyed agree that "being true to their values and beliefs makes a person cool." Because of this strong desire for authenticity, some research institutions have called Generation Z True Gen.[1]

The Gen Z preoccupation with authenticity—which has driven them away from traditional celebrities in favor of more intimate social media and YouTube influencers—makes them scrutinize the motives of large brands, presenting a challenge for today's marketing and communications professionals.

The desire for authentic communication plays into how Gen Z receives advertisements, with 84% of Gen Z reporting that they trust a company more if they use actual customers in their ads.[2]

While the mission of the church is not to sell something, many young people who walk through church doors perceive this to be the case.

Why?

Because every waking moment, someone is selling them something. In 2021, it was estimated that the average American encounters 6,000-10,000 ads a day. This is opposed to just 500 to 1600 in the 70's.[3]

It's no surprise that Gen Z is curious about the intentions of the church.

This curiosity and skepticism are personified when churches seem extremely put together and borderline perfect in their production and content delivery. The hunger for authenticity means Gen Z desires real, tangible relationships. They don't want to be sold to or be presented something.

This helps explain part of the reason for the growing micro church movement.

MICRO-CHURCH

Over the last 10-15 years, there has been a growing church move-ment toward a smaller, more organic church model. It's known by several names—the micro church, organic church, simple church.

Micro/simple/organic churches all have a few characteristics in common. They are intentionally streamlined in organization. They don't run programs, they often don't have paid staff, and they place much less emphasis on a Sunday morning service than more traditional churches do. [4]

The micro church movement has been prevalent during the Covid-19 pandemic, when churches couldn't gather in large numbers.

Part of the reason we are witnessing this growing shift towards smaller, more organic models of church is because we are seeing a transition in culture through the rise of millennials and Gen Z.

Micro churches provide a more authentic means of community. Because Gen Z is skeptical of large organizations and would prefer to shop small business over large corporations, the micro church movement appeals to Gen Z in this manner as well.

Now, I am not advocating that we all ditch our church buildings and ministry philosophies in order to adopt a micro church model. I am simply identifying that Gen Z would resonate with this sort of ministry model, and therefore we should consider ways in which we can provide authentic and small forms of ministry. For some, this may mean moving toward a micro church model. For others, this may mean integrating more small groups into their regular ministry practices.

For example, I visited Watermark Community Church in Dallas, Texas, and got to chat with some of their youth pastors. When they shared their youth ministry model, they explained that they do large youth group once a month and small groups three times a month. This runs contrary to the typical youth ministry model of once-a-week youth group.

I was surprised to hear that a megachurch was actually moving away from mega gatherings.

When I asked why, the pastor told me that recently, they discovered students would rather attend a small group gathering in a leader's home than attend large youth group. This was directly reflected in their attendance, as they saw more students attending small groups than large group.

The preference of small group gatherings is indicative of Gen Z's desire for authentic conversations and connections. In our post-pandemic age, anyone can go online and listen to a sermon from their favorite pastor. What they *can't* do online is have face-to-face conversations with other adults and students who care deeply about their spiritual and personal formation. While a Zoom small group can be helpful, the intimacy level on a screen is significantly limited compared to in-person gatherings. On Zoom, you can't lay hands on someone while you pray. You can't hug someone as they cry. You can't share a meal with your group. All of this makes small group-type gatherings even more important.

Creating opportunities for young people to engage in the church in ways other than the conventional "sit in the seat on Sunday" model will be critical for the church going forward.

"COOL CHURCH"

Generation Z's strong desire for real, raw, authentic community is having an impact on the relevant church movement.

Over the last 15 years or so, there has been a growing trend of cool or hip churches. Get rid of the pews. Ditch the choir and hymns. Add some lights, fog, and a trendy communicator, then you are on your way to attracting a younger demographic. But the movement toward a relevant or cool model of church may not work with Generation Z.

Pastor and author Carey Nieuwhof has some great commentary on this movement.

> **But we're quickly moving into a season where having a cool church is like having the best choir in town: It's wonderful for the handful of people who still listen to choral music. Something's changing. And hundreds of thousands of dollars in lights and great sound gear are probably not going to impact your community like they used to.**[5]

While we love high-production music and a relevant social media page, there are many reasons this model of church is not sustainable.

One of the reasons is simply market saturation. Many churches have a high production system, cool graphics and merchandise, and social media accounts. What was rare 20 years ago is no longer rare today; it's not unique.

On top of this, what is cool or hip is also fickle. It changes with the times. Christ and His church are anything but fickle. The almighty God is never changing. So, when a church jumps on the latest trend or fashion, Gen Z perceives the church as trying to fit in or be something they're really not.

Remember what is cool according to Gen Z? Being true to your values and being yourself. A cool church today looks more like embodying what Christ has called us to. Because when the church displays humility, proclaims the risen Christ, glorifies God, and loves their neighbor, then the church is being true to itself. That's cool.

But when we fabricate ourselves with the newest social media trend or the most popular music, this can communicate we are more concerned with outward appearances than Gospel-centered transformation, which of course, is anything but authentic.

On top of this, do we really think *we* as pastors can compete with the top social media and YouTube influencers? There are plenty of charismatic YouTube stars and captivating social media influencers that can entertain and draw a crowd of students to their platform. Gen Z doesn't need ministry leaders to try to do the same.[6]

Author and national NextGen Director of the SBC's North American Mission Board, Shane Pruitt wrote,

Gen Z really aren't looking for cool and trendy leaders to follow, they're looking for honest and authentic ones.[7]

I have found this to be true in my youth ministry as well (I know because my students tell me I'm not cool all the time).

Brett McCracken, the author of *Hipster Christianity: When Church and Cool Collide*, writes about the unstable nature of an overly culturally relevant model of church.

> **I know a few people who have stayed in hip churches for most of the last decade, but many more have moved on to another (usually liturgical and refreshingly boring) church. Others have left Christianity entirely. Turns out a church that seemed super cool to your 23-year-old self may not be appealing to your 33-year-old, professional-with-kids self...Turns out a pastor you can drink with, smoke with, and watch *Breaking Bad* with is not as important as a pastor whose** uncool holiness **might—just might—push you to grow in Christlikeness yourself.**[8]

McCracken's critique of cool church is valid. And it also speaks to part of the problem with the 70%. If we are drawing young people with an uber culturally relevant, hipster model of church that survives and thrives on its ability to stay cool, what happens when this young person graduates high school and is more concerned with raising a family and growing in likeness of Christ? All of a sudden, the hip church doesn't seem so attractive anymore. What was cool to them in high school probably isn't cool to them in their 20s. And maybe, this is part of the reason the church loses young people when they reach adulthood.

Someone once said, "What you draw them with, you will have to keep them with." In other words, whatever you are using to draw people to your church initially in order to get them in the door, you will have to continue to utilize in order to get them to stay.

This creates a form of discipleship that isn't driven by the goodness of God, but rather is driven by a constant urgency to keep people entertained. I've stumbled into this mentality a few times myself, and it's absolutely exhausting. Oh. And it's not biblical.

Relevancy matters. Sharing the Gospel in a way that speaks to young people in their cultural moment is important. But chasing relevancy to bait people into hearing the Gospel message is far from the tactics of Jesus or the early church. It was always radical love, grace, and mercy that drove people towards Jesus, not a cool factor.

PEWS, HYMNALS, AND STAINED-GLASS WINDOWS

The church where I currently serve as youth pastor was started in 1923. And like many churches which are around the century mark, there have been plenty of stylistic changes. At our church, I've heard people discuss the day pews were removed from the sanctuary. "When we removed the pews, it was like we were removing God Himself from the church," people joked. Of course, people began accepting such stylistic changes and many churches have adopted a more modern, comfortable, or cool environment. But as we've been discussing, cool doesn't necessarily resonate with Gen Z as it did for other generations.

I recently had a conversation with a senior pastor who was surprised that his 25-year-old youth pastor would frequently read from the lectionary on Sunday mornings, even though his church as a whole never utilized liturgical practices during services. He continued by saying this seems to be the trend for young people at the local Bible college.

And as I discovered, this was not an isolated personal preference, but a growing movement.

Over the last several years, there has been a steady rise of new churches that are embracing church tradition and liturgy. And the interesting part is that these churches are largely full of twenty-somethings.

The shift toward a more liturgical church setting seems shocking at first, but actually makes sense when you begin to pull back the layers.

Winfield Bevins of Asbury Theological Seminary has compiled some intriguing research in his book *Ever Ancient Ever New: The Allure of Liturgy for a New Generation and Marks of a Movement.*[9]

From Bevins' research, he discovered that what he calls "neo-liturgical" churches are successfully reaching young adults in unusual ways.

Bevins found that many young adults prefer the liturgical style of worship because of the blend of the ancient and modern.

One of the members, Susan, who is in her twenties told Bevins,

> Our worship is both formal and informal, so we
> can come as we are, yet feel a part of some-
> thing bigger than us. Through the liturgy, we
> don't have to worry about what's coming next.
> The words and prayers of the liturgy that we say
> each week sink deep into our hearts and allow
> us to worship from the heart.[10]

The feeling of being part of something bigger than us signifies the desire for church to provide an *alternative* to culture, not a reflection of it. There is a genuine longing for the church to feel different from a rock concert or a party on Saturday night.

In her article titled *Want Millennials Back in Church? Stop Trying to Make Church 'Cool'* the late Rachel Held Evans wrote,

> I want a service that is not sensational, flashy,
> or particularly 'relevant.' I can be entertained
> anywhere. At church, I do not want to be enter-
> tained. I do not want to be the target of anyone's
> marketing. I want to be asked to participate in
> the life of an ancient-future community. You can
> get a cup of coffee with your friends anywhere,
> but church is the only place you can get ashes
> smudged on your forehead as a reminder of your
> mortality. You can be dazzled by a light show at
> a concert on any given weekend, but church is
> the only place that fills a sanctuary with candle-
> light and hymns on Christmas Eve. You can snag

all sorts of free swag for brand loyalty online, but church is the only place where you are named a beloved child of God with a cold plunge into the water...[11]

Some of the markers that Evans highlights are specific to church tradition. The smudging of ashes, singing of hymns, and baptism signify something transcendent, something beyond the realm of this Earth.

What Evans calls an "ancient future community" is also an aspect of neo-liturgical church that Bevins picks up on. Bevins notes that these neo-liturgical churches display a desire to connect in a shared faith experience that reflects the early church with a connection to the past.

"Neo-liturgical worship services often feel very intimate, akin to worshipping in a living room" notes Bevins. He continues,

> Some neo-liturgical churches even design their worship space to reflect this aesthetic of intimacy by using candles, icons, tapestries, and congregational seating that is circular rather than linear. Some churches write their own songs and prayers to embody the embrace of both old and new. Written prayers are one way neo-liturgical churches involve the entire church body in worship, by allowing various members to come forward and offer prayer on behalf of the community of faith. Some churches also have prayer stations, crosses, and designated

places in the sanctuary where people receive prayer during the service.[12]

So maybe the hunger for a more traditional model of church among Gen Z isn't so surprising after all. The atmosphere that Bevins describes is one that bleeds authenticity. It displays a real, authentic form of community that involves congregants taking part in the order of service.

Here, the church isn't pretending to be someone they're not. It doesn't include the most modern worship or audio/visual elements that you might find on social media. But it humbly displays the transforming power of Jesus and leads people into a Christ-centered community. It's what the church is all about.

To be sure, I am not saying that *all* members of Gen Z, or even a majority, would prefer a liturgical church setting. Although, if millennials are any indicator for how church preferences may be trending among young people, we could see this shift even greater among Gen Z.

According to a 2014 study, Barna found 67% of millennials chose the word "classic" to describe their ideal church. By contrast, 33% prefer a trendy church as their ideal. When asked to choose their preference between a church sanctuary and a church auditorium, 77% chose sanctuary.[13]

In response to these results, vice president of *Aspen Group*, an architecture company that designs churches writes,

> **They don't want something created artificially for them; they don't want a bait and switch.**

What they want is something deeper and more authentic.[14]

Should all of our churches deconstruct our ministries and buildings in order to reflect this generational change? No. That's not what I'm arguing.

In fact, I'm still a proponent of providing high-level production with lights and music during service on Sunday mornings. And I think there's a place for that which engages a certain portion of the population. But I also think that there is another portion, perhaps a younger portion, that doesn't identify with this model.

Such a generational change should prompt us to check our level of authenticity in all areas.

For these young people, cool doesn't matter. Or maybe it does. And they think church—a stripped-down, humble, raw, authentic church—is cool.

THE AUTHENTIC CHURCH

If authenticity matters, how can we cultivate an authentic church community?

The Christian faith in and of itself is authentic.

Think about it.

To be a Christian, you must believe you are inherently sinful. You must be real about your flaws and mistakes. And you must believe that there is nothing you can do on your own to fix your sin. The work of Christ on the cross enables us to live in newfound freedom. We no longer have to be ashamed by our sin, because we have been made new in Jesus.[15] Therefore, Christians have all the reason to be genuine and authentic. Adam hid because he knew his faults and felt shame.[16] But because of Jesus, we no longer have to hide. We can be real, honest, and authentic.

It's easy to say, "Be real, bro," but it's another thing to actually BE authentic. So, I want to include some tips on how to create authentic content as shared by Hamutal Schieber, founder of Schieber Research and council member at *Forbes*. Keep in mind, this is coming from a business perspective, but I think the tips on authentic content can translate to the church arena.

Schieber defines what authentic content is:

> **Authentic content is content that is organic to the creator, and not externally imposed upon him/her. Gen Z consumers will detect a lack of authenticity and lose their trust in the creator/ influencer.[17]**

The criteria for authentic content:

- **Passion** – something the creator (whether a person or a brand) is truly passionate about, for example, speaks to the creator's values and beliefs, or solves a problem in the creator's life. Passion cannot be faked, but it is infectious. Brands can share their own passion with the creator by explaining why the brand's values are in line with those of the creator's, why they developed the product or service and how it is different than other solutions.

- **Knowledge** – the creator needs to show knowledge and expertise in the matter, whether from self-experimentation, professional experience, or even theoretical research. Brands can empower the influencers beyond just inviting them to experience and experiment with their propositions, by providing them with exclusive information and "behind the scenes" view that will differentiate the influencer from others.

- **Originality** – authentic content has to be engaging, high-quality original content. Copying content can not only be considered as inauthentic, but can also enrage young consumers, who look for fairness in content distribution.[18]

Unfortunately, part of the problem with authentic communication is that most people *assume* they appear authentic. Grab a young person in your church after you preach a message or lead a small group discussion. Ask them if you come off as genuine.

It is often specific body language that tells people whether you are being authentic or not.

- If you are smiling the whole time you are preaching, this is unnecessary—and weird.

Unless you smile 24/7 when off stage, young people will be questioning your motives, even if your motivations are pure.

- If you sound like Billy Mays advertising Oxi-Clean (how can someone be THAT excited about a stain remover?) you'll come off as a salesperson. If you are excited about what you are sharing, be excited! Be passionate! But if your job is to tell guests where the bathroom is, you probably don't need to go full-on Oxi-Clean. If you are excited ALL the time about EVERYTHING, young people will feel like you are being ingenuine.

The bottom line is, be you. Be who God designed you to be.

To quote the great philosopher Dwight Schrute,

> **Before I do anything, I ask myself, 'Would an idiot do that?' And if the answer is yes, I do not do that thing.**[19]

Ok, remove the word idiot and ask yourself, "When I'm on stage, is this something *I* would do?" If not, don't do that thing.

Now obviously when we preach, we do things we normally wouldn't do: We are probably more expressive, maybe more passionate (especially if we are talking about Jesus!), and likely our message is more thought out. But generally speaking, try to behave in ways that are natural to who God created you to be.

Authentic communication coming from the pastor or ministry leader speaks volumes to Gen Z.

JP Pokluda, lead pastor at Harris Creek Baptist Church in Waco, Texas, shares the importance of authenticity in his book, *Welcoming The Future Church.*[20]

Pokluda shares a story about a time when he had fallen into sexual temptation and looked at an image of a woman for longer than he should have shortly before he was planning to preach to "The Porch", a 7,000+ young adult ministry in Dallas.[21] Instead of starting the sermon off the way he had planned, Pokluda shared his recent slip-up into sin. He confessed in front of thousands of young adults and repented right then and there. He then continued on with his sermon. What happened next took Pokluda by surprise.

Pokluda explains he had never seen a line so long with people waiting to talk to him about the sermon. People shared that they had never heard a pastor say anything like that before, and they even confessed their own sin to Pokluda.[22]

Such a bold act of authenticity helps young people to relate to the speaker and feel connected on a personal level. They no longer feel like they are being sold to, but instead they feel like they can trust the guy on stage.

Not only does authenticity allow the audience to better connect with the speaker, but sharing weaknesses helps make the speaker more human.

Someone once said, "When we share from our strengths, we build walls. But when we share from our weaknesses, we build bridges."

Sharing our weaknesses, although painful at times, bleeds authenticity that will connect with young people.

We know that Gen Z longs for real, authentic connection. They are skeptical of large organizations that might be trying to sell them something. Instead, they want organic and authentic connection that breaks down walls and invites them into community. Churches that embrace this shift and provide opportunities for young people to connect with their church will help them come to know Jesus and grow in their spiritual walk.

There is a difference between being cool and relevant.

Relevant makes the Gospel feel approachable and understandable.

Cool makes the Gospel feel shallow and unnecessary.

Gen Z needs relevant and authentic Gospel proclamation, not a cool version of it.

REASONS FOR LEAVING:

- The church is often perceived as inauthentic, producing a barrier between Gen Z and the church.

- A lack of authenticity in the church results in a lack of trust for Gen Z.

STEPS FOR REACHING Z:

- Shift from presentation to conversation. Eliminate programs and messages that feel impersonal or shallow.

- Speak with passion and vulnerability. Sharing weaknesses highlights the human nature of the speaker, allowing Gen Z to connect on a deeper level.

CHAPTER 9

THE **PRESENT** IS KING

Author and Seminary Professor David Livermore believes there is a growing sentiment among Americans that history is "more or less irrelevant."

In his book, *Cultural Intelligence*, he writes,

> As Americans, most of us know very little about the past, and we don't care. In our minds, we don't need the past. What we are interested in is the now, the moment, and the existential experience. All we need is pragmatic problem solving. That is the vision, or lack of vision, we've taken on as a country.[1]

Because the present moment is king for Generation Z, what happens when we don't feel connected to God in the present moment? What happens when life gets busy, students graduate, head off to full-time work or college, and God doesn't seem real at the moment?

For many young people, the power of the present dictates reality. "If I don't feel close to God *now,* why would I continue going to church?"

When talking about culture, you always run the risk of overgeneralizing. There are certainly many members of Generation Z who have a resilient faith that looks further than just the present moment. But because so many young people make decisions based on their current personal experiences, the present is given precedence over the past.

The argument seems to be, "The fact that God was real years ago doesn't do much good for me if God isn't real in my life *today.*"

If you've followed Jesus at all, you know there are times when God doesn't appear to be abundantly present. In fact, there may be days, weeks, and months where God seems to be anywhere but near.

However, the author of Hebrews writes,

> **Jesus Christ is the same yesterday and today and forever.**[2]

The unchanging God never leaves us or forsakes us. Feeling that God is not as near now as He once was is not a result of God's behavior, but a result of our own wandering hearts.

We trust that God hasn't chosen to move away from us, but more likely that *we* are the ones who have put Him on the back burner. And we also know that feelings don't always represent reality. Just because we don't *feel* God's presence right now does not mean He is not with us. The transcendent reality of God is greater than our fleeting emotions and feelings.

But for a young person, this reality may be hard to grasp, and difficult to remember.

The supremacy of the here and now causes young people to question what *was* based on their feelings of what *is*.

Tessa, a writer and member of Generation Z explains,

> **Young people today have grown up in a culture that places the individual as the highest authority...and individual feelings often trump facts.**[3]

This worldview has dramatically impacted the way Generation Z interprets what is real.

In our day of postmodernism, reality is no longer concrete. Truth is relative and the individual gets to write their own story, no matter what science or reason has to say about it.

In the evangelical church in America, Christian apologetics has been a significant area of focus. Groups like *Answers in Genesis, The Truth Project,* and people like Sean McDowell have provided some excellent resources for people to defend their faith. But more recently, we have seen a shift in how young people understand reality. The rise of experientialism has created a dynamic where "my experience" is king. Like Tessa said, "Individual feelings often trump facts."

So, an apologetic that defends specific *facts* about God and the authority of the Bible is no longer sufficient. It is helpful, but we need more than this. Many young people uphold that the Bible is true and that God is real, but because of personal experiences, they no longer attend church.

I have a friend who, up until recently, was a self-proclaimed atheist. Just last week (as I am writing this) he gave his life to Christ (and we are celebrating!). My friend said that he never had any intellectual struggles with faith. His atheism was not a result of some unexplainable aspect of Christianity. Instead, he said he didn't believe in God because of his *experience* with other Christians. It was this experience that represented ultimate truth and objective reality.

The Apostle Paul wrote,

> **And if Christ has not been raised, our preaching**
> **is useless and so is your faith.**[4]

For some young people, they are saying, "Christ has been raised, I just don't care." Or "Christ has been raised, but my personal experience with church has shown me that this Christ is not worth following."

As followers of Jesus, we need to remember that for many young people, their experiences will be held in the highest regard. And in response to this, we can say, "Well your feelings don't matter."

Or "That's not the way it works!" Or insert whatever form of a disagreeing comment in response to experientialism.

OR, we can seek to listen to their experiences and understand their perspectives. Empathy is key. We can help young people recognize that there is objective truth within the Scriptures *and* there is a God who created you, loves you, and desires the best for your life. We can share *our* experience following Jesus, which will speak the language of Gen Z's worldview. And we can call young people to remember the times where they have experienced God before and remind them that He will be faithful again.

It is possible to empathize with the feelings of young people while *simultaneously* reminding them that God does not change even though our feelings do. But shutting down their feelings is a quick way to communicate you don't really care how they feel and neither does God.

NEW LIFE EXPERIENCES

The season of life where students are likely to leave church is one where their past experiences are sometimes uprooted and replaced with new, more exciting experiences.

The 70% statistic is tracked during the most tumultuous time in the life of a young person.

Once a student graduates from high school, they often enter the workforce full-time or head off to college. Both of these scenarios likely include moving out of their parent's home into their own place of living.

This newfound freedom results in a life where the 18-year-old gets to start "their own life" so to speak. No longer will mom and dad be keeping a curfew or make you get up for breakfast.

All of a sudden, present reality is detached from the systems and structures that life revolved around for 18 years.

One of these systems and structures is the church itself.

Young people naturally detach from their church if they physically move to a different city or state. Whether or not the recent grad goes out of their way to find a new church community in this tumultuous new stage of life is completely up to them.

For many young people, they passively fall away from church, they don't aggressively exit it. This explains why statistics show many people who leave church do not leave their faith completely.

Then *why* do they leave, even if the circumstances for an 18-year-old *do* make it challenging to find a new church community?

Part of it, I believe, is because of the power of the present.

The present moment—moving away from home, living in a new city with new roommates—is a new, exciting reality. So past moments where God *was* present in one's life are not as important as the present reality that one is *now* living in, because the present has taken precedence.

So where do we go from here? How do we lead young people into a resilient faith that doesn't crumble amidst their new stage of life?

THE ART OF REMEMBERING

If you were asked, "Why do you believe in God?", what would you say?

Maybe you would talk about the authority and truth of God's Word. Maybe you would mention that you believe because of His sacrifice on the cross. And for some of us, we believe in God because we have experienced His power and have been personally transformed by Him.

When I was a couple of years into youth ministry, I went through a season of deep anxiety and depression.

For whatever reason, this fear of preaching took hold of my life. The night before I would preach, I remember being curled up in a ball with my eyes full of tears. I trembled at the thought of getting on stage and speaking, for no specific reason at all. Just plain fear. Hours before I preached, I would look in the mirror and see red splotches on my face and neck. I was so scared to preach that my body was physically reacting to this fear!

This is when a wise pastor told me, "Reese, if God has called you to ministry, you might have to do it scared." This wasn't what I wanted to hear, because I wanted God to just take the fear away.

But that didn't seem like it was going to happen anytime soon. So instead, I preached scared out of my mind. For months, this fear controlled my life.

Each time I preached, however, the fear lessened. I began to feel more confident and assured whenever I got on stage.

Today, I feel zero fear at all when I get ready to preach. Of course, I get butterflies sometimes, but fear no longer has power over me.

For me, this is an *only God* moment.

The fact that I no longer face fear when I preach could have only been accomplished by the power of Jesus Christ. I know this because I had come to the end of myself and had no hope, I could get over this fear. So, the fact that I *did,* showed me God worked a miracle in my life.

Today, when I am faced with a difficult situation, when there is a conflict with a parent or student that seems unreconcilable, or when I'm doubting my own giftings, I remind myself of the time God gave me the victory over my fear of speaking.

One of the ways we combat this *present is king* worldview is by looking to the past.

In the book *Faith for Exiles*, the Barna group conducted research on what the most important aspects are to a robust faith in Jesus for young people. They found that those who are deeply committed to following Jesus have had a *personal experience* with God.[5]

In other words, students with a strong faith could name a time in their life where God moved in such a way that they knew He was real. These personal experiences are not some "mystical" moments, but rather they are times students encountered the power of the Holy Spirit in their lives. I'm guessing you have had some of these moments too.

For those who have left the church, have they simply forgotten the moments where they experienced the real presence of God?

Have they forgotten the time where God answered their prayer or healed one of their friends?

Have our young people failed to remember the love and affection they felt from God during worship?

Maybe this is thinking too simplistically.

Could young people really be leaving our churches because they have simply forgotten about God's impact on their lives?

I think this is actually quite possible.

Why?

Because in a very real sense, this was *exactly the same problem* with the Israelites. Their walking away from God often came down to one single source: Forgetting.

The Israelites failed to remember God's faithfulness in their life.

And if this was the problem with the Israelites' faith, couldn't it be the problem with a generation overly focused on the present and forgetful of the past?

Like we discussed previously, when God brought the Israelites out of Egypt, He removed them from 400 years of bondage and slavery. God sent remarkable plagues and literally split the Red Sea, while throwing the greatest military in the known world into the water. An experience of such power and providence would be one hard to forget, right? I guess not. Because shortly after the parting of the Red Sea, the Israelites were worshipping a golden calf and doubting God's promises.[6]

So, what does God do? He calls His people to *remember*. He reminds the Israelites of His faithfulness in Egypt.

Over 28 times in the Old Testament, God speaks to the Israelites using the phrase,

> **I am the LORD your God, who brought you out**
> **of Egypt, out of the land of slavery.**[7]

Why? Because God knows the power of transformational experiences. For the Israelites, the crossing of the Red Sea marked the power of God and the love He had for the Israelites. This event was a transformational experience for the Israelites because they experienced God in a personal and profound way.

But God also reminds us because He knows that we humans easily forget. We get caught up in our present circumstances and believe that the most recent feelings we have are closest to the truth. We disregard God's past work in our life as somehow less valid.

Just as God reminded the Israelites of their experience at the Red Sea, we should remind ourselves and our young people of their experiences with God. Remembering the past gives our faith confidence for the future.

John Piper notes the connection between the memories of past grace and the confidence in future grace when he wrote,

When gratitude for God's past grace is strong, the message is sent that God is supremely trustworthy in the future because of what he has done in the past. In this way faith is strengthened by a lively gratitude for God's past trustworthiness.[8]

In ancient Hebrew culture, one of the chief spiritual failures was forgetfulness. And because of this, the primary goal of Hebrew education was fostering the remembrance of God.[9] We should be asking ourselves today, "How can we foster a community of remembrance in our churches?"

One of the tangible ways we can lead people in the art of remembering is during Sunday church service. What if we thought of church services as calling our people to simply remember the goodness of God through worship, teaching, and prayer?

When we walk into the sanctuary, we are reminding ourselves of God's faithfulness in our lives. Here, we enter into a historic reality, where we recall the faithfulness of God and remember He is the same today.

Our personal faith does not start from square one when we enter church. If we haven't felt near to God lately, it isn't because we've lost our faith. We do not have to go looking for God again as if He has wandered away. We do not have to attempt to reach God through our efforts and obedience. Instead, we enter into a place of remembrance where we are reminded of all the times God has been faithful, both in the Scriptures and in our lives personally. Here, we find comfort, hope, and peace.

Parents, I would encourage you to write down the times when your kids experience God in a profound way. Write down the times when God has answered a prayer for your kids or when they have seen God move in their life. *Then as God often did with His children,* remind your kids of these moments, that they will be continually reminded of God's power and intimacy in their life.

When young people question God because they do not "feel close to God," gently remind them of God's presence that surpasses time and personal feelings.

As Jack Haberer wrote,

> **Faith can remember that the Spirit who made His home in your heart promised to stay, whether you feel Him or not.**[10]

Faith remembers that feelings are a real thing, but not the ultimate thing.

Make it a practice to ask people, "When was God the most real in your life?" Or "What has God been teaching you lately?" Connect significant experiences and personal growth with the work of God in their life.

An additional practical way to foster a community of remembrance is to keep a journal of answered prayers. Encourage young people to write down the times when God came through in a big or a small way. And when they begin to doubt or wrestle with their faith, remind them to go back to this journal to recall God's faithfulness. Doing this reminds students of God's power in their life and encourages them to keep the practice of remembering.

Let us not fall into the trap of forgetting as the Israelites did.

When our young people get caught up in the myth that the present always reigns supreme, remind them of God's love and faithfulness that surpasses the boundaries of time.

REASONS FOR LEAVING:

- Because individual experience is so important to Gen Z, a period of time when God doesn't seem present may be enough for them to doubt God and question the importance of the church.

- In our fast-paced, changing world, it's easy to forget God's unchanging character.

STEPS FOR REACHING Z:

- Listen to their concerns and remind them that personal feelings don't always indicate God's presence (or lack thereof).

- Encourage Gen Z to recall the times when God has been faithful before, and remind them that He will be faithful again (*Only God Moments*).

CHAPTER 10

HURT

Because experiences are so important to Gen Z, a positive church experience can be a catalyst for their faith, and a poor church experience can be detrimental.

Unfortunately, for many members of Gen Z, their church experience has been marked by negativity, pain, and even trauma.

Andy Stanley, lead pastor at North Point Ministries in Georgia, recently gave five reasons why people are leaving the church. One of those reasons is, "They had a bad church experience."

Relationships are messy and complicated. But if our actions are rooted in Jesus' command to love one another (John 13:34), we can prevent many of the experiences that lead people away from his body.[1]

There are numerous ways in which people have felt hurt by the church community. But one of the most significant forms of hurt causing young people to leave the church is that of sexuality.

In *You Lost Me: Why Young Christians are Leaving Church...And Rethinking Faith*, the Barna Group gives six reasons why young people are leaving the church. Here is one of them:

"Young Christians' church experiences related to sexuality are often simplistic, judgmental."

Barna states,

> **One of the significant tensions for many young believers is how to live up to the church's expectations of chastity and sexual purity in this culture...Research indicates that most young Christians are as sexually active as their non-Christian peers, even though they are more conservative in their attitudes about sexuality.**[2]

The way culture talks about sexuality is degrading and harmful. But the tactics the church has used to teach sexuality isn't setting up young people with a sexual ethic all that different from their non-religious peers.

An aspect of Christian sexuality that has received significant pushback lately is that of purity culture.

PURITY CULTURE

The term "purity culture" is often used to define the Christian sexual ethic that promoted abstinence and modesty, especially among youth.

The "True Love Waits" program, which began in 1993, headlined the rise of the purity movement. As the movement grew in the '90s, estimates of teenage adherents reached as high as 2.5 million worldwide. Youngsters wore purity rings, signed purity pledge cards and attended purity balls, with girls dressed in white and escorted by their fathers.[3]

From the 2021 New York Times article *"How an Abstinence Pledge in the '90s Shamed a Generation of Evangelicals"* to the #ChurchToo movement on Twitter, news outlets and individuals have been sharing their experience with the harm caused by Christian purity culture.

Among those who helped launch the Christian purity movement in the '90s was Joshua Harris. His 1997 book *I Kissed Dating Goodbye* sold roughly a million copies. In his writings and speeches, Harris advocated for courtship relationships and warned teenagers of the dangers of dating, especially dating that would lead to any physical intimacy.

And while his book was impactful for many Christian teens and parents, Harris also discovered a dark side to his book. The book exercised fear and shame to motivate young people to abstain from dating and sex. Harris found that using fear as a motivator often drove young people *away* from God, instead of towards Him.

Joshua Harris eventually pulled his book from circulation and apologized for the role he played in causing anyone feelings of shame, fear and guilt. Today, he no longer considers himself a Christian. It's a sad story, and one that has multiple layers to it that we don't have time to unpack here. But Harris' story rings true for many Christian teens who have been raised in the church and eventually walked away.

In her book, *Pure: Inside the Evangelical Movement That Shamed a Generation of Young Women and How I Broke Free*, Linda Klein describes the purity movement as the following:

> **It was all about how [a woman] needed to be a good Christian by protecting [men] from the threat that is you—the threat that is your body by wearing modest clothing and keeping mind and body free of sex until marriage.[4]**

For Klein, purity culture thrived on its ability to shame young people into abstinence.

One common practice at youth retreats was to pass around pieces of chewed gum to illustrate to young women if they failed to remain pure, this is how they would appear to a Christian man looking for a godly wife.[5]

Is this how Jesus or Paul, or anyone in the Bible talks about sexual purity? Comparing God's creation to chewed gum that nobody wants?

This is not the narrative that the Scriptures speak of. The identity marker of Christianity has always been love, not fear. As we read in 1 John,

> There is no fear in love. But perfect love drives out fear, because fear has to do with punishment. The one who fears is not made perfect in love.[6]

When *love* is the driving factor, we desire sexual purity because we love God and want to please Him. We see sex as a gift that we can look forward to within the confines of marriage.

But when *fear* is the driving factor, we desire sexual purity because we don't want to become "used goods" in the eyes of God or a potential spouse.

Sure, fear is *a* motivator. It's just not a good motivator.

There are, of course, many beneficial aspects to the purity movement.

The movement was created in order to help young people consider God's design for marriage and sex. When we teach purity that isn't built on fear and guilt, but rather on the promise and freedom found in Christ, young people will receive the beautiful meaning of God's intention for dating, marriage, and sex.

The heart is the key factor in this conversation.

When leaders are teaching sexual purity, are they doing so with a motivation to scare young people? Are they encouraging young people to stay away from sex because of the pain and damage it will cause them? Or because it is God's best for their life that is a result of Christ's freedom, love, and sanctification in our lives?

For many young people, exposure to purity culture has caused them to question the necessity of the church community.

Now, to be sure, have some young people left the church simply because they no longer want to be held to a Christian ethic and would rather live according to their own standards? Absolutely.

This will always be part of the challenge when sharing the Gospel. In our Western individualism, we feel as though nobody has the right to tell me what to do or how I should live. There will *always* be people who reject the Gospel due to their unwillingness to surrender their earthly desires under the Lordship of Jesus. In this sense, the Gospel is "offensive" by itself. So why would we make the Gospel *more* offensive by piling on condemnation, anxiety, and fear? We can teach Biblical ethics without fear. We can teach young people to wait until marriage without shaming them. Let it be the Gospel itself that drives people away, not our poor proclamation of it.

Not only is this fear mentality completely contrary to Scripture, but it's emotionally exhausting.

It forces people to tip-toe through life, wondering when they are going to step on the next spiritual landmine. But Purity Culture is just one of the many ways young people have experienced pain and hurt at the hands of the church.

LGBTQ

As the conversation around LGBTQ[7] rights becomes more prevalent in our culture, the church's response becomes increasingly important.

And while many Christians might think this issue isn't a problem within *their* church, they should reconsider.

According to a recent Gallup study, one in six Gen Z adults identifies as part of the LGBTQ community.[8] Gen Z is the most sexually diverse population ever—a defining characteristic for this generation.

If you have a youth group with over 10 students, odds are someone there identifies with the LGBTQ community.

This means that the church needs to be equipped to have conversations with people about sexuality and faith. "Being gay is bad" is poor theology and ineffective discipleship. The conversation around LGBTQ and the church is much more complex, and we certainly do not have the space to unpack all of this here.

How the church responds to issues surrounding the LGBTQ community will help shape Gen Z's perspective of Christianity.

Unfortunately, we've dug ourselves into a bit of a hole (or crater) over the past few years.

In *UnChristian*, David Kinnaman and *Barna Group* analyzed the results of a 2006 survey among a random sample of 16- to 29-year-olds.[9] The study found that the top three attributes young

Americans associated with "present-day Christianity" were being antigay (91%), judgmental (87%), and hypocritical (85%).[10]

While this study is well over a decade old, these numbers give us a general idea of what young people think about Christianity.

The fact that the first attribute given is "anti"-anything should alarm us. We have become more famous for what we are against than what we are for. The "anti" church is the image many people have of the evangelical church today.

And for many young people, the church's treatment of the LGBTQ community has been a factor for them leaving the church.

According to a 2016 study from the Public Religion Research Institute (PRRI), young adults (age 18 to 29) who left their childhood religion are about *three times more likely* than seniors (age 65 and older) to say negative religious teachings about and treatment of the gay and lesbian community was a primary reason for leaving their childhood faith (39% vs. 12%, respectively).[11]

These findings indicate that young people are increasingly concerned with the church's relationship with the LGBTQ community. And so far, the church's negative attitude (whether actual or perceived) toward this group has driven many young people to leave the church.

But what about LGBTQ *Christians* who have left the church?

Andrew Marin, in his book, *Us Versus Us: The Untold Story of Religion and the LGBT Community,* provides some rather shocking data.

Out of the 1,712 LGBTQ people interviewed who left the church after the age of 18, only 3% say they left primarily because of the church's belief that same-sex marriage was wrong.[12]

The primary reasons given for leaving were "Do not feel safe" (18%), "Relational Disconnect with Leaders" (14%), and "Incongruence between teaching and practice" (13%).[13]

In other words, the vast majority of LGBTQ people who have left the church did not leave because of a doctrinal position on gay marriage, but because of how they were treated.

One individual interviewed for this research named Sally, a lesbian living in San Diego, says she quit going to church years ago.

> I felt lost. I never gave up on God because I believe in God's promise to love me and execute justice on all those that really hurt me. Though I'm also ready to accept God's final judgment possibly against me because I believe it will be just. So my problem isn't with God, it has always been with the institution that allows those who claim to obey God and yet make me feel most alienated.[14]

Personally, I have spoken with multiple young people who would identify with Sally. They aren't willing to give up on God, but they feel just about done with church.

If the 3% statistic wasn't surprising enough, try this:

76% of LGBTQ people are open to returning to their religious community and its practices.

Compare this to statistics released by the Barna Group, where only 9% of Americans are open to returning to faith and its practices after making a decision to leave their faith community.[15]

So according to the data, LGBTQs are open to returning at a rate *65% higher than the average American.*

What would it take for them to return to church?

Those surveyed said they would return to their faith community if they "felt loved" (12%) and were "given time" (9%), among other answers.[16]

Only 8% said their faith community would need to change their theology in order for them to come back.

Eight percent. That's it.

When I first discovered these numbers, my response was shock, sorrow, and then hope.

I was surprised that so many members of the LGBTQ community left the church for reasons *other* than theological disagreements. Oftentimes, it is easy for us to write off certain individuals from the church because we think they just don't like our beliefs. That's far from the case here.

It's one thing if Jesus or the Bible drive people to such negative conclusions about Christianity, but it's another if our unkind thoughts, words, and actions do.

Second, I felt sorrow. I felt sorrow for those members of the LGBTQ community who had felt unloved, unimportant, and unhuman. These image-bearers were often made to feel less than by other image-bearers.

But I also felt sorrow for Christ's church. The very people who were supposed to be creating spaces for those on the margins to receive the good news of the Gospel were forcing people into the margins, away from the hope and abundant life promised by Jesus.[17]

And finally, after seeing these shocking statistics, I felt hope.

Hope because somehow, after being mistreated and unloved, *many* members of the LGBTQ community would consider returning to church. And they wouldn't consider returning only if we changed our doctrine, but often, they would return if we started loving them like Jesus called us to.

It seems so unlikely and yet, this is the story of the Gospel, right?

Broken hearts.
Lost people.
Loving God
Radical Redemption.

It's possible. But only through the grace of God.

I want to suggest that in order to reach members of the LGBTQ community with the Gospel, we don't need to change our orthodox Christian beliefs about sexuality and marriage.

To be sure, there will be a segment of the LGBTQ population who won't feel comfortable attending church unless its theology is open and affirming.

But for many, a change in theology isn't required in order for them to return. But what *is* required of us is humility, love, compassion, forgiveness, courage, and trust.

Radical things, maybe. But biblical things. *Jesus* things.

CARING FOR THE HURTING

When you google "reasons why people leave the church," you will get a variety of results. In many of these lists, there is at least a mild suggestion that these reasons are not reasonable.

For example, when someone names their "bad church experience" as a reason for leaving, this is often met with,

Well, that's not a good reason to leave the church!

And, while this assertion may be true, that Christ's church is more important than a bad experience, it is insufficient for discipleship, biblical community, and, well, compassion.

I've heard someone say it like this:

Let's say that you were bitten by a dog growing up. Before this incident, you had a relatively positive view of big dogs but after being bitten, you feared them. And eventually, this fear spread to all dogs. No matter how many times other people told you that their dog wasn't dangerous or that their dog was friendly or not to "throw the baby out with the bathwater" you still experienced an involuntary fear reaction when seeing a dog.[18]

Now some people may be able to recover quickly from this sort of experience. But for some, it may take years to overcome their fear.

If we apply this scenario to church, we can see how a traumatic experience may cause someone to avoid all things church. But the issue is when we suppose this fear of church is a choice, as if someone is actively sinning against God because of their traumatic experience.

If you have a fear of dogs, could you imagine someone telling you that you need to confess your grudge against dogs?

The sentiment to "pull yourself up by your bootstraps" after a traumatic church experience isn't loving, nor is it going to encourage those young people to stick around at your church. An approach that invalidates someone's pain conveys that we care more about being right than we do about caring for the body of Christ. But according to Scripture, we can't even claim we are "right" when we respond in this sort of way.

Paul reminds the church:

> **If one part suffers, every part suffers with it; if one part is honored, every part rejoices with it.**[19]

Our role as individuals within the body of believers is to share joys *and pains* with one another. One member's painful experience should be felt by the entire body in a way that seeks healing and restoration.

While we need to teach our young people to have resilient faith that surpasses the unkind words and actions of another Christian, we also need to empathize and listen to their traumatic experiences.

Instead of responding with "don't throw the baby out with the bathwater" when it comes to a bad church experience, we can ask people to share their experiences with us so we can walk alongside them.

The pains experienced in this world are not meant to be dealt with individually, but rather within the context of the local church.

> **Bear one another's burdens, and so fulfill the law of Christ.**[20]

When the church functions as Christ intended it to, we will care for those who have had painful church experiences. We won't neglect them or shame them. We will also encourage them to still be part of the biblical community.

The topic of sexuality and the treatment of the LGBTQ community is just one of the many reasons people have had painful experiences in church.

People have experienced pain from church members in many other forms, not just in the category of sexuality. But the key to all of this—the solution—is a Christ-centered response that listens, empathizes, forgives, encourages, and restores.

This may take time, even time away from the people who caused the hurt. And if there has been serious mental, emotional, or spiritual trauma, a counselor should be sought out.

But the step toward healing begins when the church embodies the characteristics we have been called to.

Put on then, as God's chosen ones, holy and beloved, compassionate hearts, kindness, humility, meekness, and patience.[21]

REASONS FOR LEAVING:

- Negative experiences within the church often result in doubt, pain, and trauma. For many, church is associated with these negative traits.

- The church is considered "anti-gay" which turns off young people.

STEPS FOR REACHING Z:

- Sit down with some young people in your church and ask them to share their church experiences. Listen, empathize, and bear their burdens. Walk alongside them in discipleship, encouraging healing and restoration.

- Talk openly about LGBTQ issues within the church. Consider preaching a sermon series on faith and sexuality where you can explain how a Christian should respond to our LGBTQ neighbors.

CHAPTER 11

A CATALYST CALLED DOUBT

When young people think about their faith, the Bible, and following Jesus, one of the most natural inclinations they have is doubt.

While we've discussed the 70% of high schoolers who leave the church after they graduate, there is another 70% statistic that fewer people are aware of.

According to the Fuller Youth Institute, 70% of high school seniors have doubts about their faith.[1] The reality is, most young Christians *do* experience doubts, they just don't always express these doubts out loud.

Part of the reason for this is that Generation Z doesn't believe the church is a safe place to express their doubt.

Going back to Barna's brilliant research for *You Lost Me,* one of the six reasons young people give for leaving the church is, "The church feels unfriendly to those who doubt."

Barna explains,

> **Young adults with Christian experience say the church is not a place that allows them to express doubts. They do not feel safe admitting that sometimes Christianity does not make sense. In addition, many feel that the church's response to doubt is trivial. Some of the perceptions in this regard include not being able "to ask my most pressing life questions in church" (36%) and having "significant intellectual doubts about my faith" (23%).[2]**

Sadly, less than half of those young people who experience doubts about faith actually shared those doubts with an adult or friend.[3]

It makes sense that a majority of young people would have doubts about faith in our current cultural moment. In previous generations, there was a general trust that surrounded religious institutions. But today, the natural lean for Gen Z is skepticism when it comes to religious institutions. According to Springtide Research Institute, Gen Z gives the church a 4.9 out of 10 on a level of trust.[4]

Additionally, the rise in the spread of misinformation on social media means for every fact about faith, the Bible, and Jesus, someone out there is providing an alternative answer that doesn't represent truth.

As one journalist wrote on the subject,

> **For every fact there is a counterfact and all these counterfacts and facts look identical online, which is confusing to most people.**[5]

No wonder Gen Z has some doubts about their faith. They encounter all sorts of crazy theories concerning Christianity online.

Is the vaccine the mark of the beast?

Is the next president the Antichrist?

Was Jesus actually a disciple of Muhammed?

(I found these online, so they MUST be legit.)

Unlike their millennial predecessors, Gen Z grew up in the smartphone age, essentially born with an iPhone in hand (slightly kidding), with 98% of them currently owning a smartphone.[6] This means that it is easier than ever for young people to access information, as well as *misinformation*. It should be expected, therefore, that Gen Z will come across information that challenges their faith beliefs.

However, the perception that "good Christians don't doubt" is often expressed by churches and youth ministries. While this is sometimes unintentional, this notion can inhibit students from expressing their doubts, especially in the context of their church community.

But when talking about doubt, it's important to note that doubt is not the same as unbelief.

Genuine unbelief is a complete rejection of the Faith or some part of it. Meanwhile, doubt is a state of questioning, rather than a rejection.

Researcher and Professor Irene Cho said, "Doubt is not what kills faith. Silence is."[7]

In other words, the doubt itself is not as dangerous as the silencing of those doubts. This is critical for parents, teachers, and church leaders to understand.

When a young person approaches a youth pastor or a parent or a teacher and asks, "Why did God let all those people die in the forest fires last summer?" Or, fill in whatever tragedy. And we respond with "Oh, we don't ask questions like that." Or, "Just trust Jesus. He is the answer."

What that communicates is:

1. The church is not a safe place to ask questions.

2. God isn't big enough to answer my difficult questions.

When we don't allow young people to express doubts in the context of family or faith community, guess where they will express doubts? With their friends or in secular institutions. I would much rather walk with a student in their doubt in the context of other believers than let them wrestle with the doubt on their own.

One of the best answers we can give to difficult questions comes in the form of four words. *"I don't know, but."*

"I don't know, but why don't I talk to some friends and we can sit down over a cup of coffee and chat more about this?" Or *"I don't know, but* that is a great question. Let me think about this and we can discuss it together."

Kara Powell of Fuller Seminary notes that an "I don't know" from an adult does not communicate ignorance, but it communicates that even as adults, we don't have all the answers, and that's ok. It also communicates that you don't have to have all the answers in order to follow Jesus.[8]

Jesus didn't say, "Come to me, all who are smart and are self-assured." He said, "Come to me, all you who are weary and burdened, and I will give you rest."[9] God's power is made perfect in weakness. This frees us up from having to know all the answers.

THE DOUBTER

If I asked you, who is the most prolific doubter in the Bible, what would you say?

I'm guessing most of you would say Thomas. The guy is literally called "Doubting Thomas."

Here is the section of Scripture in John 20 that gets Thomas his nickname:

> So the other disciples told him (Thomas), "We
> have seen the Lord." But he said to them, "Unless
> I see in his hands the mark of the nails, and place
> my finger into the mark of the nails, and place
> my hand into his side, I will never believe."[10]

Later, Jesus walks in, goes right up to Thomas and says, "Put your finger in my wounds."

At this point, Thomas has got to be thinking, "Alright Jesus, this is kind of weird, but alright if you say so." Thomas places his finger in Jesus' wound. Check out Thomas' immediate reaction:

> **"My Lord and my God!"[11]**

MY LORD AND MY GOD. He made the most powerful declaration of the deity of Christ found in any of the Gospels.

Thomas' doubt is what leads to his belief. Because he doubted, he discovered. Because he doubted, he approached Jesus. Because he doubted, he professed Jesus as God.

This is why it is critical we create spaces for our young people to ask questions and to express their doubts in the context of biblical community.

The odds are, students in your church have doubts, they just probably aren't expressing them. One of the ways we can encourage those in our churches to wrestle with difficult aspects of their faith is by first and foremost modeling this ourselves. If we as the leaders and pastors appear to never wrestle with some of the difficulties of Scripture or never share any doubts, why would our congregation?

Many times, an anti-doubting culture can be implicitly formed rather than explicitly adopted. It seeps into churches with subtle comments of academic arrogance and assuredness on theological matters. This slowly communicates to people that if you disagree with the widely accepted beliefs of the church, it won't be well received. We need to create cultures that uphold sound doctrine while still allowing platforms where people can disagree, question, and doubt.

At our church, one of the ways we have tried to foster a culture where students can ask questions is through our "Don't Ask That" series. The idea was that we would talk about questions that normally might be met with a "Don't ask that" response in church.

I met with a group of our students to think through some of the hardest questions that students wrestle with in terms of their faith. We did six different sermons, ranging from "Why does God let bad things happen to good people?" to "What does God think about gay people?"

After each message, students sat around in small groups led by a couple of adult leaders where they could process what they heard and even express their own doubts and questions. Leaders were encouraged to welcome students who vocalized their doubts and keep the conversation going, rather than simply shut it down with the *correct* answer. This was by far the favorite series for our students all year, and we are making it a yearly tradition.

Let's finish this chapter with good old doubting Thomas.

Thomas is only mentioned one other time in the Scriptures after His interaction with Jesus. We don't really get much else out of Thomas or know what happened to him, until Hippolytus and Eusebius wrote it down around 200 AD.[12]

It is widely accepted by scholars and historians that Thomas went and took the Gospel to other people groups. He shared the Gospel in India.[13] It is believed that he reached more people groups and went further with the Gospel than any other apostle. He preached the Gospel until he was martyred on a mountaintop in 72 AD.[14]

He went from doubting Thomas to missionary for the Gospel.

There is power in our doubt, because when we express our doubts, we often grow in our faith.

The story of Thomas, no matter what he went on to do after his encounter with Jesus, should encourage us to let students wrestle with their faith and struggle with their doubts. We know God is big enough to answer their difficult questions, even if we are not.

REASONS FOR LEAVING:

- Church is perceived as an unsafe place to express doubts.

- Doubt is often understood as the opposite of faith, making young people feel alienated if they have doubts.

STEPS FOR REACHING Z:

- Encourage young people to share their doubts and struggles. If they don't feel safe expressing these doubts in church, they will find another place to do so.

- Normalize doubt by sharing your own faith struggles with Gen Z when preaching and having personal conversations.

CHAPTER 12

KILLING THE
BRAND

In *Hidden Worldviews: Eight Cultural Stories that Shape our Lives,*
Steve Wilkens outlines the cultural values that we have adopted as
Americans.[1] One of these values, Wilkens believes, is influencing
the worldview of Christians more than any other: Consumerism.

If we retrace our steps a bit, we will see how the church has
adopted some of the aspects of American consumerism.

At a basic level, consumerism is an idea that encourages the acqui-
sition of goods and services in ever-increasing amounts.[2] While
this definition of consumerism is alive and well in the American
church, I want to consider the more subtle notions of consumerism and how they have seeped into our programs and ministry
philosophies. Christianity has a long history with consumerism,
which cannot be traced to one single source.

In Colleen McDannell's *Material Christianity: Religion and Pop Culture in America,* McDannell argues that Christianity's absorption with consumerist culture is long-standing but has accelerated in more recent years to create the "production of Christianity."[3]

When talking about this consumer mentality being implemented by the modern church, it's hard to find a stronger example than the megachurch model of Willow Creek.

Willow Creek Community Church, founded in 1975 by Bill Hybels just outside of Chicago, created multiple elements of engagement to reach a specific individual. This individual was called "Unchurched Harry."

Harry was a template for what the average person in the Chicago suburbs looked like, and what he was looking for in a church.

For Willow Creek, the first step in reaching someone is to understand them—how they feel and think, what they need and how they will respond. If a new idea or concept can't pass the "Harry test" (in that it would appeal to and attract Harry) it doesn't go far in ministry strategy conversations. In some ways, Unchurched Harry is in the driver's seat.[4]

It should also be noted that this sort of thinking and strategy is not inherently bad in and of itself. Doing cultural exegesis—discovering the culture of unreached people in the area and creating ways to communicate the Gospel to reach them—is actually strategic evangelism.

Our American culture has created an individual that wants high production, entertainment, and comfortability. So, Willow Creek capitalized on these characteristics, creating a church culture that reflected many of these Western ideologies. But when this methodology feeds the American beast of consumerism, you end up with a church philosophy that starts to resemble a commercial more than the cross.

The more extreme example of Willow Creek's consumer-oriented ministry philosophy is Robert Schuller's 78,000 square foot church in California called the Crystal Cathedral. Schuller advertised his church as a "shopping center for God."[5] Ultimately, the church went bankrupt and collapsed in the early 2010's. This caused many to question if the church that combined Christianity with American consumerism marked the end for consumer-driven churches.[6] While many members of Gen Z seem to be fed up with such a model of church, some churches still carry the undertones of American consumerism.

CONSUMER CONTENT

Willow Creek had a creative way of appealing to the consumer, specifically in the way they drove their content.

One of the methods Willow Creek utilized to appeal to Unchurched Harry was that of multimedia on Sunday morning. Sophisticated lighting, sound and visual imagery are all a prerequisite in this media age. Implementing high quality media provided a high production experience for Harry.

Additionally, Willow Creek used theater to kick off the sermon. According to one study on Willow Creek:

> The five-minute drama that winsomely intro-
> duces the theme of the day is being increasingly
> utilized by churches concerned about effective
> communication."[7]

Today, an excellent sound system, great music, and comfortable church buildings are the norm. But for the 70s and 80s, this was innovative. Consider how performing arts played a central role for Willow's services according to *Christianity Today*:

> The classical form of art in churches, beside
> architecture and paintings, has always been
> music—hymns, choirs, classical performances—
> but that shifted under the influence of the Willow
> seeker-friendly service. The shift underway (and
> WCCC was a part, perhaps a big part) was from
> *worship to performance*, from congregational
> singing to solo performance, from choirs to
> 'worship bands.' Hymns were devalued and up
> the charts rose praise and worship songs.[8]

Notice the shift from corporate worship to performance-based worship.

The reason I am highlighting Willow Creek here is because they are one of the innovators of the "seeker sensitive" church model.

In 2007, Willow published a study titled *Reveal,* which was made up of 6,000 survey responses by Willow Creek attenders.

What they found?

The seeker-sensitive model does not work.

By and large, Willow Creek attendees reported feeling "stalled" and "dissatisfied" with their faith. The seeker-sensitive model *did* benefit those who were "exploring Christianity." But those who were "close to Christ" were stalled in their spiritual journey.[9]

The problem isn't that Willow tried to make the Gospel accessible to the unchurched. The problem is that the unchurched began to drive Willow's theology. Willow Creek became obsessed with marketing spirituality to the lost.

As *Christianity Today* explains, the *Reveal* study framed the church "as if it were merely a distribution point for spiritual goods and services."[10]

What was the main way to drive the mission forward in Willow's model?

We display, you watch.

We produce, you consume.

To be fair, there will always be a level of consumption in the church. In fact, we *have* to consume God's Word.

As Jesus answered Satan in Matthew 4,

> **It is written: Man shall not live on bread alone, but on every word that comes from the mouth of God.**[11]

Consuming in this manner isn't an option.

What I'm talking about is the more passive, sitting back consumption of Christian content that doesn't require anything of oneself. This is another danger of the consumer mentality in Christian churches.

Author and preacher Francis Chan notes this distinct form of consumption that the church in the West has embraced.

He writes that these Christians remind him of "the fattest people on earth" who have consumed so much food that they can no longer walk.

> **They are fed more and more knowledge every week. They attend church services, join small group Bible studies, read Christian books, listen to podcasts and are convinced they still need more knowledge.**[12]

Francis Chan is essentially saying the American church is "fat on teaching and lean on doing." We love consuming knowledge and information, but our spiritual formation often stops here.

We usually think of spiritual formation in two distinct steps. First, I grow closer to Christ through information. I read my Bible, pray, study, listen to sermons, etc. Second, I begin to apply the things that I have learned. If I listened to a sermon on forgiveness, I put this into action by choosing to forgive my spouse the next day. This is the basic way we think of growing in Christlikeness.

But what if instruction (reading, praying, sermons) and application (living out what we've learned) are *both* part of the learning process? What if we don't just learn through knowing, but learn through doing? When we begin to think of spiritual formation as both knowing *and* doing, we won't be so stuck on information that we fail to practice this information.

Paul encourages the church in Philippi,

> **What you have learned and received and heard and seen in me—practice these things, and the God of peace will be with you.**[13]

For Paul, practicing what you have learned is key, because in the practice, "The peace of God will be with you."

The information-driven Gospel preaches that information = transformation.

But the reality is, more knowledge and information aren't necessarily linked with a more robust faith in Jesus. Consumption of information does not always correlate to transformation.

Barna did a study in 2017 that showed those who "Love Jesus but not the church" have orthodox beliefs about the Bible, God, and Christianity. In fact, their beliefs on the Trinity, the omniscience and omnipresence of God, *do not differ significantly from those who attend church.*[14] Put simply, for those who left the church but continued in their faith, right doctrine wasn't a significant issue.

There are many students who know the Bible inside and out, and live a life committed to Jesus. But I am not sure if the *lack* of Bible knowledge is a significant contributing factor to young people leaving the church. In my experience, those who leave the church are often those who have been raised in the church, understand the Scriptures, but have left for a variety of different reasons.

My fear with the assumption that Bible knowledge leads to a transformed life and robust faith is that we will focus more on an information-driven Gospel than a transformation-driven one.

Of course, we believe God's Word is the supreme source of truth and the perfect Word of God. All that we do should be centered around the Scriptures. But sometimes we can get so caught up in getting our students to know *about* God that they leave the church without really ever *encountering* God on a personal level.

The Pharisees are a perfect example of a group of people who knew the Bible inside and out yet were not transformed by the power of the Word. They literally memorized the entire Torah (Old Testament law). Although they knew everything about God, they did not really *know* God.[15]

So, what's the problem with consumer culture?

First and foremost, it embraces a faith mentality that is more about receiving than participating. It communicates that following Jesus is about what information I can consume.

Second, consumerism developed and reached its peak in the church arena during the time when baby boomers and millennials were the ones who were trying to be reached. The "we show, you watch" philosophy worked in part because this was the type of culture that baby boomers and millennials connected with.

But unlike their predecessors, Gen Z isn't so hot on consumerism. And maybe, that's OK.

FROM CONSUMERS TO CREATORS

"Gen Z doesn't want to buy your brand, they want to join it."

This is the title from a 2019 research article indicating the shift away from consumer culture for Generation. Z[16]

This shift is one of the most significant differences we have seen from the millennial generation to Gen Z. And it is one that will have a dramatic impact on how Generation Z views the church as a whole.

According to research from the Pew Research Center, Gen Z is an increasingly socially conscious generation. They are unafraid to hold marches and rallies, which we saw clearly in 2020. They are also not afraid to use the technology that they grew up with to enact change.

Furthermore, Gen Z expects brands to take a stand on social causes and is more likely to buy from a brand that aligns itself with a cause.[17]

For example, the shoe company, Tom's Shoes, has a business model that runs on the premise for every pair bought, a pair of shoes will be donated to an underdeveloped country. This philosophy connects deeply to Gen Z because they feel like they are making a difference with their purchase.

Because of Gen Z's desire to enact change and engage with the culture around them, some have dubbed Gen Z as "Culture Creators."

Consider the info gathered from market research firm *The Wildness:*

> What we've uncovered in our research is that this is a generation of Culture Creators (CCs) that are redefining entertainment, consumption, the workplace, and marketing. The CCs are empowered, connected, empathetic self-starters that want to stand out and make a difference in the world. They have created a new Cultural Currency that values uniqueness, authenticity, creativity, shareability, and recognition. What's different for this generation is not as simple as the internet or technology. Technology is an important component, but what's changed is *this generation's relationship with culture.* In short, Gen Z doesn't want people to speak for them—they want to actively engage in the creation of meaning surrounding them, and that includes brands.[18]

This shift from *consumers* to *creators* is visible in the way that Gen Z engages with the culture around them, especially within the social realm.

SOCIALLY INVOLVED

Unlike any generation we have seen before, Generation Z cares deeply about social issues that are going on in their community and around the world. Not only does Gen Z care about problems that affect people in their community, but they actually take steps to do something about it.

Anya Dillard, a 17-year-old from New Jersey, is one of the many members of Gen Z who decided to take action during the tumultuous year of 2020. In June of 2020, she organized and led a protest in her community that drew over 2,000 people.[19] And Anya is not alone.

In 2020, our nation saw young people on the frontlines of social change. Rachel Hatzipanagos of *The Washington Post* highlights this characteristic of Generation Z, writing,

> **The political engagement of Gen Z, whether it is about climate change, racial justice or gender equality, is fast becoming a defining feature of the generation.**[20]

Although social involvement is a unique trait of Gen Z, teenagers have been at the forefront of social and religious movements for centuries.

In his book *Teenage: The Prehistory of Youth Culture,* Jon Savage traces the development of teenagers across the world from 1875-1945. One of the recurring themes in his book is that teenagers are often setting the trend for culture, participating in political and social movements, and playing a significant role in wars across the world.[21] This is also true of more recent history here in the U.S.

Del Gandio, author of *Rhetoric for Radicals: A Handbook for 21st Century Activists,* notes the similarities between teenagers in 2020 and those in the civil rights movement.[22]

> When we think about the 1960s, it's often marked by radical activism, radical social change, and often led by the youth. I think that's sort of what's going on now.[23]

But while social change has often been part of the teenager DNA, Gen Z seems to value social engagement even more than their teenage predecessors. And it goes beyond racial protests.

Regarding the differences between the baby boomer generation and Gen Z, The *New York Times* columnist Nicholas Kristof notices:

> Doing good is no longer a matter of writing a few checks at the end of the year, as it was for my [baby boomer] generation; for many young people, it's an ethos that governs where they work, shop and invest.[24]

This distinction Kristof identifies is key. For his generation (baby boomer) the primary way to enact change was through financial giving (passive). But for Gen Z, enacting change takes place through involvement and participation (active).

One simple way our youth ministry has utilized this generational shift is by engaging cultural issues with faith practices. For example, when the war between Russia and Ukraine broke out, we hosted a youth prayer night. Two of our Ukrainian-born students who normally aren't super involved in our youth ministry showed up and participated. This was a huge win because it gave students space to join together in prayer about current issues they cared about.

Even if you disagree with where Gen Z is placing their efforts politically or socially, Christians should be encouraged by Gen Z's desire to be the change they want to see in their communities.

MEDIA CREATION

Another way we have seen a shift from consumers to creators is through Gen Z's involvement with media.

For years, the American media designed content for its users to consume. Think Hollywood, cable TV, and more recently, Netflix. While these three media giants are still relevant today, they are not nearly as pervasive within the younger generation. For example, Gen Z watches TV 10% less than their millennial predecessors. Additionally, Gen Z relates more to creators than traditional celebrities. Consuming content is not as attractive as creating it or engaging with it.[25]

Seventy percent of teenage (Gen Z) subscribers say they relate to YouTube creators more than traditional celebrities. Social media creator content performs far better than traditional celebrity content on the same channels. Even more impressively, social media creators get 12 times the number of comments that a traditional celebrity does.[26]

While millennials may be called the "consumer" generation, Gen Z is the "creator" generation.

As with social issues, Gen Z doesn't want to watch (passive), they want to participate (active).

One of the ways this is illustrated is through the uprising of the social networking service, TikTok.

While some people are satisfied with simply viewing content, many others desire to contribute and create content of their own. TikTok dances are the new trend partly because it involves direct engagement, where the viewer can attempt the dance, prank, or stunt they see on TikTok or create their own version.

We know that Generation Z is the most tech-savvy generation yet, so what are they doing when they're using their device? According to The Generation Z Study of Tech Intimates Report, more than half of Gen Z respondents (52%) are creating and sharing content with others. Not only are they personally engaging with content (by creating their own) but they are corporately engaging with content by sharing it with others.[27]

The shift from simply consuming content to wanting to create and contribute to the culture around them is significant for the church to understand.

Canadian Pastor Carey Nieuwhof boldly states,

The gap between how quickly you change and how quickly things change is called irrelevance. The bigger the gap, the more irrelevant you become.[28]

Much of my research has suggested that young people aren't leaving the church because it lacks truth, but because it lacks relevancy. And one way the church can be relevant for Gen Z is by engaging creators instead of only consumers.

GOSPEL PARTICIPANTS

The good news in this generational shift is that a mindset which is more concerned with *joining* a cause than it is consuming information is more theologically in line with Scripture.

The call of the Gospel is ultimately an invitation to participate in God's redemptive plan for humankind.[29] It is to engage with God and one's neighbor in a loving relationship.[30] It is to actively pursue the will of God in all things,[31] that we may see God's Kingdom come in our lives as individuals[32] but also that God's Kingdom may invade the social structures and our society as a whole.[33]

In the most basic sense, the great commission is a call to GO. To engage. To relate. To create disciples of Christ.

The fact that Generation Z *actually wants* to engage in something rather than just consume something should be viewed as a positive shift for the people of God.

The Gospel has never been about just consuming information or knowledge, but rather actively participating in God's Kingdom Mission here on Earth. This is good news for the church.

So, can the church embrace this generation shift from "consumer to contributor" in its philosophy of ministry? I think there are a couple ways that it can.

REASONS FOR LEAVING:

- Church is consumer-driven, so Gen Z (creators) struggle to connect with God and people in meaningful and transformative ways at church.

- Church programs seem out of touch with cultural and social issues.

STEPS FOR REACHING Z:

- Provide spaces within the church for Gen Z to creatively participate within the body of believers.

- Capitalize on Gen Z's social awareness by creating opportunities for young people to be the change they want to see in their communities.

CHAPTER 13

ENGAGING ~~CONSUMERS~~ CREATORS

With this dynamic shift from consumer to creator culture, we have to ask the question, how can we design ministry experiences to better engage creators?

Vince Parker, who oversees the youth ministry at all of Life. Church's 41 campuses, has identified this shift in culture.[1]

I once heard Vince say, "I don't want a student-*attended* youth ministry. I want a student-*owned* youth ministry."[2]

I love this. Because students want to be the change in the world and desire to actively engage with culture, giving young people ownership allows them to live out their faith in practical and meaningful ways. One of the strategies for creating a student-owned youth ministry is by implementing a student leadership team.

YOUTH MINISTRY LEADERSHIP

In our youth group, the design for the student leadership team really comes out of Ephesians 4:

> **And he gave the apostles, the prophets, the evangelists, the shepherds and teachers, to equip the saints for the work of ministry, for building up the body of Christ.**[3]

The student leadership team is a tangible way of equipping the saints and giving them opportunities to lead and make disciples in the process. We want our students to consume the Word of God, but we also want them to put this consumption into action by serving their church body as outlined in Ephesians 4.

To give you an idea of what this looks like, our student leadership team is comprised of five different, smaller teams, which are led by spiritually mature upperclassmen. This places the responsibility of these teams on the students themselves, so they can personally disciple other students on their team.

We empower our students to have significant responsibility for running the youth group. Students lead worship, tech, choose and organize games, design merchandise, run our social media, lead prayer gatherings before service, and plan large events. We also meet regularly to talk about how the various teams are working and how we could improve.

The risk here is that you put students in charge who aren't personally or spiritually mature enough to lead. This is why all students on the leadership team fill out an application and go through an interview process. Constant feedback is also key, so students can understand where they are crushing it and where they might need some improvement (once again, discipleship opportunity).

There are many benefits in a student leadership team. But perhaps the most significant benefit is that it teaches students that their faith is active, not passive. Following Jesus is not about what you can get (consume), but about what you can give.[4] We grow the most when we're in the game, not when we're sitting on the sidelines.[5] I found this to be true for students in our youth group, as many of them are challenged with uncomfortable tasks like sharing their testimony, discipling someone younger than them, and organizing and leading teams.

All of this, I believe, helps students connect their faith to the meaningful mission of seeing their peers come to know and grow in Christ. Here, they are *participating* in the mission of Jesus, not passively *attending* youth group.

The practice of giving students leadership opportunities in the church is a specific method that the Fuller Youth Institute identifies as being critical to seeing young people engage in the church.[6]

Fuller Youth Institute's *Growing Young* project set out to ask why certain churches grow in their ministry with young people. One of the commitments of churches that were "growing young" had in common was the practice of keychain leadership. In other words, they were exploding with staff, volunteers, and parents who help their church flourish by handing over the keys of power, access, and ability to their students.

The concept of keychain leadership is described in *Growing Young* as the following:

> Often the persons who are most trusted in an organization are given a set of keys to the building. Those people also hold the most power—they can literally decide to let people in or to keep people out. Keys provide access to physical rooms, as well as to strategic meetings, significant decisions, and central roles or places of authority. The more power you have, the more keys you tend to possess.[7]

Keys represent a physical form of power, but they also symbolically represent something bigger. *Growing Young* continues,

> No matter how many 'keys' you hold (whether physically or symbolically), if you are willing to entrust your keys of leadership to young people, they will trust you with their hearts, their energy, their creativity, and even their friends."[8]

And if you are in youth ministry, if you are a leader or a pastor, I'm willing to bet someone once gave you a set of keys. Someone took time to invest in you, to empower you, which helped launch you into faithfully following Jesus and leading others. Similarly, passing on keys to those younger than us helps them feel empowered, equipped, and trusted to do the work of the ministry.

1 Timothy 4:12 reminds us,

> Don't let anyone look down on you because you
> are young, but set an example for the believers
> in speech, in conduct, in love, in faith and in
> purity.

Giving young people in your church an opportunity allows them to be this example to others.

We've talked about student leadership, but how do we create experiences that engage Gen Z creators in actual church services and ministry programs?

CREATOR-DRIVEN SERVICES

It's interesting that over the course of the last century or so, the church service as we know it has not dramatically changed. We have things like the Jesus Movement of the 1960s, which helped launch the contemporary worship phenomenon.[9] But the order and the norms of Christian worship services have remained relatively unaltered.

Consider this outline of a typical church service in the 2nd century from N.R. Needham's *2,000 Years of Christ's Power: Age of the Early Church Fathers:*[10]

Part 1: Service of the Word

1. Opening greeting by bishop and response
    by the congregation. Often, the bishop
    would say "The Lord be with you" and the

congregation would respond, "And with your spirit."

2. Old Testament Scripture reading. Usually read or chanted by a deacon.

3. Psalm or hymn (I). Chanted or sung.

4. New Testament Scripture reading (I). This first NT reading was from any NT book outside the Gospels.

5. Psalm or hymn (II).

6. New Testament Scripture reading (II). From one of the four gospels.

7. Sermon. Delivered by the bishop, while seated.

8. Dismissal of all but baptized believers.

The service would conclude with silent prayer, the Lord's Supper, and a benediction given by the deacon.

So, 2,000 years ago, the church had a welcome, Scripture reading, worship, and a sermon. Apart from a few variations, this is basically what our churches do today.

It's amazing to think of all that has changed throughout Christianity over the last 2,000 years.

Consider the fact that we have managed to translate the Bible into over 1,300 languages.[11] We have numerous different translations and versions of the Bible in order for the modern reader to better comprehend God's Word. Or think about the boatload of ministries churches have today; from men's ministry, women's, youth, marriage, recovery, etc.

But remarkably, our worship services have remained similar throughout the last 20 centuries. Most churches today still have a greeting, a reading from Scripture, and a few songs. And to be sure, there is nothing *wrong* with this model.

If we are able to translate the Bible while still holding the authority and the accuracy of God's Word, we need to ask if we can also translate worship styles in order for people to be able to uniquely glorify God and better grow in their relationship with Him.

I am certainly no expert in this arena, and I am definitely (just ask my wife) not a worship pastor. But historically, the church has always sought to move believers forward in their relationship with Jesus, even if this means trying something new.

OK, I know what you're thinking.

Why should we reinvent the wheel? The church has been worshipping this way for 2,000 years for a reason.

True. There is great value in our long-lasting Christian tradition. We should not seek to throw everything out and change all we have ever known about worship services.

As Scott Cormode wrote in *The Innovative Church,*

> Every Christian's faith depends on the inherited
> Christian tradition. We receive the faith; we do
> not invent it.[12]

While we don't invent faith, we do innovate our practices. As our youth are leaving the church in waves, we need to at least re-think and re-imagine the way we worship.

The church I used to be a part of in Oklahoma City, Life.Church, has a core value that their team often communicates:

> We are faith-filled, big-thinking, bet-the-farm
> risk takers. We will never insult God with small
> thinking and safe living.[13]

Life.Church practices what they preach. They are often trying new things to translate the Gospel in a unique and fresh way, while still holding to strong and unchangeable biblical truths. For example, Life.Church created the YouVersion Bible App in 2008. Who would have thought 2,000 years ago that people would be reading the Bible on a digital screen the size of a slice of bread? Crazy.[14]

OK. Your church may not have the resources to develop an app, but that's OK. What I'm getting at is simply *starting* to think outside the box. And thinking outside the box can mean shifting our attention from performance to participation.

Pastor Zach Lambert of Restore Austin says that he believes *participation* is the key to attracting and engaging Gen Z to any sort of spiritual activities.

> **We've seen a hunger in Gen Z for more experiential stuff—something they get to participate in rather than receive. They want to belong to a community rather than an audience.**[15]

While people would think that Gen Z would be the most likely demographic to watch church online, Lambert is not finding this to be true.

Lambert continues,

> **Online is complete audience. You can't even create a facade that it's participatory. I think that's why you're seeing a drop in participation during COVID.**[16]

The fact that the most tech-savvy generation of all time doesn't watch church online as much as other generations indicates that there's something deeper going on. I believe this development is linked to the fact that online church lacks participation and personal experience. It is completely passive, and this doesn't connect with Gen Z. Thinking through how we can engage Gen Z at a participatory level will be crucial if the church wants to reach young people.

Many of you reading are parents, pastors, teachers, leaders, and believers in the next generation. If you are anything like me, you don't have time to completely reinvent the wheel and change the way your worship services look. So, I wanted to give you a couple of simple, practical ideas to help engage the *creator* culture that is Gen. Z.

CREATIVE WORSHIP

One of the things we have tried in our own youth group is designing unique ways for students to worship. We provide art stations across the auditorium and our worship team will play a couple of songs. Students can sit at their seat and pray, they can stand and worship, or they can express themselves in worship through creative art.

Some of our students will illustrate their emotions and their love for God through artwork. This might be a picture of parents arguing, and a cross from heaven cutting through the noise to represent the presence of God shining through brokenness. The best part of this is that no artwork will be exactly the same. Students are free to create (which we know many of them are more apt to do) their own expression of worship through art.

This also shifts the feel of the service from a consumer mentality to a creator one. Because Gen Z desires to participate and engage with culture around them, giving students opportunities to do just this helps them connect with God in more personal and inti-mate ways. Giving young people the opportunity to create shows that there isn't just *one way* to worship God. The people of God are unique, and our worship can be too.

The reality is, we worship God differently and uniquely all the time. We just don't do it in church.

All of us would agree theologically that worship is not limited to singing a certain number of songs, reading Scripture, and listening to a sermon. It certainly includes these elements, but it is not limited to them. The definition of worship is the expression and adoration for God. We have many different ways of doing this.

In the well-known film, *Chariots of Fire*, Olympic runner Eric Liddell explains, "God made me fast, and when I run, I feel His pleasure."[17] Our giftings, when used to glorify God, are an active expression of worship. We worship God uniquely outside of church, so why not incorporate some of these elements inside of church?

Once again, this is easier said than done, so let's continue with some practical examples.

METHODS OF ENGAGEMENT

Former youth pastor Dr. Ron Marrs has manufactured multiple different worship experiences for young people. In regards to youth ministry, Ron always said, "If I was going to fail, I was going to fail creatively." And for Ron, one of the creative things he implemented included services where he would preach a message out of one of the Gospels, then students would act out the story of that specific Gospel, almost like a drama.

And mixing up your worship services in order to allow students to *create* rather than *consume,* doesn't even have to be this drastic.

Sometimes during my messages, I will have 2-3 students sitting on stage with their Bibles taking notes. Each time I get to a passage of Scripture, I'll ask one of those students to read that portion.

This does a couple things. First, it allows students to have a voice within the sermon itself. Second, it communicates to everyone else that students have a role to play in the reading and sharing of God's Word. Finally, and maybe most importantly, it allows for more of a dialogue within the sermon and less of a monologue.

Students are literally monologue-ed to death (OK maybe not literally). But think about it. They are often talked at by parents. Talked at by teachers. Talked at by coaches. They are told what to do all day long. While still being a place of strong biblical teaching, what if we included more opportunities for students to speak instead of being talked at?

Let's be clear. The monologue form of teaching isn't going away. Jesus taught in monologue format all the time. And some of the most powerful truths I have learned have come from a regular, monologue sermon. But other truths are ones I picked up from watching, participating, or experiencing. So, the question isn't "Should we do monologue sermons?" Rather, the question is "Should we *only* do monologue sermons?"

Recently, our youth ministry team implemented what we call "Culture Creators." Three weekends out of the month, we do our usual teaching with a monologue-style sermon. But the fourth weekend, we provide a space for students to think critically and creatively about their faith in a practical, hands-on manner.

The teaching session for "Culture Creators" consists of students seated in small groups around the room. Students are presented a case study of sorts where they need to come up with a response to a contemporary issue in culture. Students might be given a scenario where they have to have a conversation with someone who disagrees with their views or beliefs. Or we might tell students to provide a Christian response to something like "Cancel Culture" or another hot button issue in our world.

Students then spend 20-25 minutes thinking critically and conversing with one another about how they would respond to such a situation. They are encouraged to use Scripture, but they don't have to. Each group has 1-2 adult leaders at the table to help facilitate the conversation, but the leaders are not to provide their own personal insight. Instead, students are encouraged to share openly, even if their opinions may be misguided.

If students think their ideas will be shot down, the whole thing fails. The goal is that students feel like they are in a safe environment where they can express their beliefs in a personal way.

Ultimately, the aim is not to come to the perfect answer for each case study. "Culture Creators" is less about being right and more about giving students an opportunity to think critically and practically about their faith.

At the end, I will approach the topic from stage and share my own biblical perspective for 5-7 minutes. Students then have five more minutes to turn to their groups and adjust their conclusions based on the biblical teaching on the issue. This is the place for leaders to help guide the conversation to a biblical conclusion.

"Culture Creators" provides an alternative, hands-on method of learning. It challenges students to engage in an active way where they think about how their faith intersects with everyday life.

In his book *Spiritual Formation as if the Church Mattered,* James Wilhoit explains,

> Christians must feast upon truth, and yet (teaching) is only one discipline in an array of activities that Christians need to participate in to grow in the likeness of Christ.[18]

Said another way, transmitting truth via teaching from the pulpit is one way to share truth, but it is not the only way. We see Jesus teaching to crowds, but we forget the teaching He did while demonstrating and sharing experiences with the disciples. Both forms of teaching are valuable.

TEACHING FOR TRANSFORMATION

Not only does participatory style teaching engage creators like Gen Z, but it's simply better for overall student retention.

Studies are conclusive that all people, but particularly students, retain the *least* amount of information through a monologue form of teaching.

According to a study by the *National Training Laboratory,* students retain 5% of information given through the format of a lecture. Using audio/visual methods bumps the retention up to 20%, while demonstration raises the retention to 30%.[19]

The time when students retain the most amount of information is when participatory methods are used. Group discussion puts retention at 50%, practicing the information by doing bumps it all the way up to 75%, and the greatest form of teaching for students' retention is when students teach others (90%).[20]

There are a couple of important things to note regarding this study.

First, the lowest form of retention rate (lectures) is the one most often used in churches today. And second, this study complements the trend of Gen Z, who connect deeper when they are active participants.

A study done at Xavier University further backs up the superiority of active learning over the lecture method.

> **After the implementation of active learning strategies, the teacher researchers concluded that a moderately positive change occurred concerning retention of essential concepts after teachers converted from traditional lecture methods. The teacher researchers reported that incorporating active learning techniques in their classrooms encouraged cooperation, improved student engagement, and decreased unwanted behaviors.[21]**

Active learning helps young people retain and internalize what they are being taught. It takes more creativity and preparation for the leader, but it's worth it. Another facet to consider for teaching young people today is attention spans.

A recent study by Microsoft concluded that the human attention span has dropped to eight seconds—shrinking nearly 25% in just a few years.[22]

Does this mean people only listen to the first eight seconds of your sermon, then fall asleep? No, not necessarily. People *are* capable of paying attention longer than eight seconds, but they will become increasingly distracted as time wears on.

The response to decreasing attention spans has been to shorten the sermon length. Years ago, a normal sermon length would be 45-60 minutes. According to Pew Research, today the average pastor preaches for 37.[23]

Tim Keller, widely known for his expository Bible teaching says,

> **In general, I think for most Sunday congregations the sermon should be under 30 minutes. That's safest. If you are a solid preacher but not very eloquent or interesting it should also be shorter.[24]**

Dang Keller. Stone cold.

While short attention spans may be cause to shorten our sermons, it is not an excuse to be unengaging. Just because people may be more likely to zone out during a sermon doesn't mean we're off the hook for designing engaging sermons.

Andy Stanley makes the argument that short doesn't always equal more engaging. Stanley explains that kids can remember a three-hour movie after watching it once. And not only do they remember the movie, but they can also recite many of the lines.[25]

Why?

Because the movie is engaging. It captures the viewers' attention.

I think both sides of this argument are valid.

Preaching a 45-minute sermon might not engage Gen Z in a meaningful way. *However,* a creative, engaging 45-minute sermon with thoughtful preparation and sound biblical teaching probably will.

The bottom line?

Short attention spans aren't an excuse to preach short sermons without solid biblical truth. This isn't a sermon. This is glorified entertainment.

On the other end, the nature of your audience's attention span shouldn't be ignored. If your goal is translating information, then go for as long as you want—people just won't be listening. But if you are going for *heart transformation,* then consider how to share God's Word in a way that will sink deep within the heart of the congregation so they can remember and be transformed by the Holy Spirit through your preaching.

Being creative in the way we present the Gospel message helps us engage people past a shallow, consumeristic level.

In all, consumer culture is a dangerous ideology for the church to practice and participate in.

It communicates that the church is more about receiving information than it is about participating in the mission of Jesus. As I indicated earlier, consumer-driven church models were incredibly effective (despite their clash with a biblical model of church) for *previous* generations. And while Gen Z still holds some of the consumeristic traits of its predecessors, they are far more creator/contributor-driven than consumer. They don't want to passively consume a product; they want to actively join and engage with it.

And for the church, it is critical that we think through some of the ways we can allow Generation Z to engage with the Gospel in formats that are unique and meaningful to them.

REASONS FOR LEAVING:

- Because Gen Z learns best in interactive ways, the monologue sermon format often feels boring or out of touch.

STEPS FOR REACHING Z:

- Create experiences where Gen Z can learn hands-on. During sermons, be creative with how you present biblical truths through formats like demonstrations, conversations, and group activities to maximize retention.

CHAPTER 14

CHANGES

"We gotta make a change. It's time for us as a
people to start makin' some changes... You see,
the old way wasn't working ..." [1]-Tupac Shakur

I'm pretty sure Tupac wasn't thinking about the church when he
wrote these lyrics, but anyone wanting to make some changes
can identify with his words.

The problem is, change isn't easy.

Many of us would rather keep things as is, especially if everything
is going well. The "if it ain't broke don't fix it" mentality works
as long as things aren't broken. And to be sure, the church *isn't*
broken. But just because something isn't broken doesn't mean it
couldn't use refining. The fact that a majority of Gen Z leaves the
church when they graduate is reason enough to do a deep examination and make some changes in our churches.

But where do we start?

Change often starts when awareness begins.

AWARENESS

As soon as I began analyzing the strengths and weaknesses of our youth ministry, I was motivated to implement practical changes that would magnify our strengths and address our weaknesses.

One night after youth group, my wife and I were reflecting on the night. We thought about all of the students who walked into youth group with different burdens, pains, and hurts. We then thought about how there really isn't a space for them to share intimately with others. They were told to come in, sit down, shut up, and listen. Listen to the worship, listen to the message, maybe play a game, then go home.

It felt... shallow.

I know that one in six Gen Z teens suffer from major depression.

I know that one in 11 Gen Z high schoolers have attempted suicide in the last 12 months.[2]

Think about how many of these students walk into youth group every night, only to walk out without having a meaningful personal interaction. This prompted us to start dreaming about how we could fill this void.

DREAMING

What if we could incorporate teaching the Gospel into a personal interaction format, where students weren't passive listeners but active participants? Here, they would be encouraged to share their struggles and wrestle with their faith on an individual and corporate level.

That night, Culture Creators was born.

But that idea was only born out of awareness. We realized that we were failing to meet the needs of many of our hurting students. And more than that, we realized that we were only teaching the Gospel through a monologue sermon, which was not connecting with all our students on a deep level.

Someone once said, "The first step toward change is awareness. The second step is acceptance."

Once we became aware of these shortcomings, we began to dream about what could be.

VISION

Unfortunately, many of us operate our ministries in echo chambers that lack various perspectives and church traditions. The result can be a failure to objectively assess one's ministry, which leads to a reluctance to change.

Put simply, we don't initiate change because we don't know change is actually possible, and tangible. We are so accustomed to what *is* that we don't consider what *could be*.

How do we dream about what *could be*?

Once I started talking to other youth pastors and even visiting their youth ministries, my eyes were opened to different perspectives and unique ministry practices. This is part of the beauty of the "Capital C" church. God gave His church different leaders with unique giftings and abilities. Sharing ideas with other leaders helps all of us consider *what could be* in ministry.

There are SO many amazing resources out there for pastors and leaders today. We really don't have an excuse NOT to keep growing and learning.

But with so many resources out there, how do we know which ideas to implement and which to toss out?

I'd say a couple of things.

First, does this idea add to your mission?

Carey Niewhof said,

> **Most people opposed to change do not have a clearly articulated vision of a preferred future. They just want to go back to Egypt. And you can't build a better future on a vision of the past.**[3]

Leaders think most people are opposed to change when in reality, people are opposed to change without a vision for the future.

Pointing people to the mission and vision, *what could be*, begins with clearly articulating where you are trying to go.

In our youth ministry, our mission is "Leading students to become fully-devoted followers of Christ." If a program, ministry, or new idea doesn't contribute to this mission, we don't do it. Period. If there is no clear mission, you will be tempted to become all things to all people, implementing every new strategy, stretching your ministry thin, and confusing your volunteers and parents.

The second thing to ask when considering a new idea is, is this idea biblically sound?

I would hope that if the idea contributes to your mission, it's also biblically based. This seems obvious, but I have seen so many ministries implement strategies that seem more like relevant marketing techniques than biblical evangelism. Is this new idea contrary to anything in Scripture? If it is, don't do it. It's not worth it.

Third, pray about it.

Maybe the idea adds to your mission and maybe it's biblically sound, but maybe it's not God's timing. Or maybe, God is simply calling you to do something else. I can recall a time in my ministry when a certain direction checked all of the practical/strategic boxes, but when I went to God in prayer, the answer was "wait," and eventually "no."

Fourth, pitch the idea to your team.

Pull in some high-capacity students and volunteers and ask them if they think this idea will help push the mission forward. Just because YOU think an idea will work, doesn't mean the rest of your team will think so. One time, I came to our leaders with a small group concept that had worked in previous youth ministries I had been a part of. But when I shared the idea, it became clear that more than half of our team was not on board with this philosophy. Ultimately, we decided to go a different direction.

Additionally, just because an idea sounds good to a group of adults doesn't mean it will connect with your students in the way you think that it will. I'm always surprised when decisions are made *for* students without consulting *with* students. Turns out the game you did in Young Life 20 years ago might not be fun for a student today. Ask them.

IMPLEMENTATION

If we understand our strengths and weaknesses (awareness), creatively consider the possibilities (dreaming), and know if an idea is worthy of application (vision), the final step is putting the idea into action (implementation).

This is the fun part.

It's scary putting a new idea into action if you *haven't* done the previous steps. But if you have, then you can move forward with the confidence of God and the confidence of your team.

I think about when Moses was commissioned by God to lead the Israelites out of Egypt. When God gave Moses the vision, Moses was worried that the Israelites would not be supportive.

Moses said to God,

> Suppose I go to the Israelites and say to them,
> 'The God of your fathers has sent me to you,'
> and they ask me, 'What is his name?' Then what
> shall I tell them?[4]

Like we often do, Moses felt the fear of rejection and failure. But because He had been in the presence of God, He was able to move forward with God's plan in confidence, despite his fear of rejection and lack of speaking skills.

After you have completed the previous steps, you may still be hesitant to implement a new idea. But that's OK. You now have the backing of your team; you've spent time with God; you can move forward.

And hey. The idea could still completely fail. Who knows?

Like Ron Marrs said, I'm of the opinion that if I'm going to fail in youth ministry, I'm going to fail creatively. I'd rather go all out trying to reach the next generation for Jesus than sit back and do the same thing we've always done, hoping for a different result in young people leaving the church.

When you go to implement a new idea, make sure you are specific and practical. Write out exactly what you are going to do, minute by minute. Now it's not just a new idea, but it's a practical reality. If you want to execute, make sure you are incredibly specific with your expectations.

Just because you are going to be creative with the chance of failure doesn't mean you get to be haphazard. Be intentional.

If we are serious about reaching Gen Z with the Gospel, then we need to critically examine our church and consider the aspects that need changing. Of course, change can be hard. But it doesn't have to be. When we are clear about our vision, focused on our mission, and relentless in our pursuit of God, then HE will bring about the right changes in our church. Here, change isn't scary. It's exciting.

CHAPTER 15

THE FUTURE
CHURCH

To close, I want to pose the question, "What is the future of the church?"

Well, if 50-70% of Generation Z is leaving the church, this would lead us to believe that things aren't looking too hot for Christianity. And for years, people have believed that as the world progresses through time, as the world becomes more educated, that religion will decrease.

However, sociologists are finding quite the opposite.

Recently, a study was conducted by the Pew Research Center and the *Washington Post* subsequently ran an article titled "The World Is Expected to Become More Religious—Not Less".[1]

The article notes that in America and Western Europe, the percentage of people without religious affiliation is rising for the time being. However, across the globe, religion is growing steadily.

While we have been primarily discussing the status of the church of America, we need not lose sight of what God is doing throughout the world.

The research findings predict that in the decades to come, Christians and Muslims will make up an increasing percentage of the population, while the proportion that is secular will shrink. Experts predict that by 2030, China will have the world's largest Christian population.[2] And by 2050, Africa will be the first continent to reach one billion Christians.[3]

Statistics also show that atheism has peaked. There are fewer atheists in the world today (138 million) than there were in 1970 (165 million).[4] Furthermore, Christianity is growing at five times the rate as atheism.[5]

Jack Goldstone, a professor of public policy at George Mason University is quoted,

> **Sociologists jumped the gun when they said the growth of modernization would bring a growth of secularization and unbelief...That is not what we're seeing. People...need religion.[6]**

Why do people need religion?

Because Jesus is the only way to human flourishing.

Secularism isn't working. Postmodernism isn't working. Individualism isn't working.

Society isn't going to progress until our planet becomes some sort of flawless utopia. Think about it. We have state-of-the-art technology, world-class medicine, unlimited entertainment options, and yet we are more depressed, anxious, and suicidal than any other generation in human history.[7] The way of man is hopeless. We NEED a Savior.

Worldwide, the Gospel is spreading. The Kingdom is advancing.

Of course, our hope isn't in statistics. Just like we won't *lose* hope when we read about the 70% of young people leaving the church, we won't *gain* hope when we read about Christianity growing worldwide. Our hope is in Christ. However, with all the negative press about Christianity dying out, it is encouraging knowing that statistics tell a different story.

We know that the future of the church is not dependent on cultural Christianity, where following Jesus is popular and widespread. The way of Jesus progresses through humility and weakness. The early church grew because of persecution, not because of political triumph.

The way of Jesus and the future of the church will progress when we embrace that we are now exiles in a foreign land. We cannot go back to the Christian America of the 1950's. We have left Kansas and religious majority, but that's OK. Because maybe, this is exactly where revival will take place. It is in the dry and desolate land that allows us to proclaim to our culture: The people walking in darkness have seen a great light; on those living in the land of deep darkness a light has dawned.[8] As the world grows darker, the light of Jesus shines brighter.[9]

AN ENCOURAGEMENT

I wrote this book because I care about young people and believe the BEST way to live a fulfilled and meaningful life is by living it for the glory of God.

But I also wrote this book because I was a bit tired.

I was tired of people telling me, "You know 70% of high schoolers will leave the church when they graduate." I was also tired of seeing so many students fall in love with Jesus but fall out of love with His church.

But this book was never intended to be a conversation ender; a "Well that's why young people are leaving the church! Now we know what to do!" The conversation is much more nuanced and complex than that.

My hope instead, is that this would be a conversation starter.

Maybe you will start a conversation at your church about the narrative of fear surrounding young people that often plagues the church.

Or maybe you will discuss the topic of doubt, and how your ministry can equip young people to wrestle with doubt.

Perhaps you will have a conversation with parents about how you can create a youth ministry that isn't system focused (think

Tebow), centered on creating youth ministry attenders, but spirit focused, centered on creating lifelong disciples.

Maybe you will have some of these conversations, or maybe you won't. And that's OK. Maybe there wasn't anything ground-breaking in this book for you, and that's fine.

But I do want everyone, whether you will use what you have read in this book or not, to leave with one thing.

I want you to leave encouraged.

In my research for writing this book, I have read every book written on Gen Z and the church. Most of the time when I finished a book, I would set it down and feel a deep sense of defeat.

As a current youth pastor, I would reflect on what I'd just read. I'd think about all the detailed research and the recommendations the author would put forward to "make your youth ministry the next biggest and best thing." As I reflected on these things, I felt overwhelmed.

Many of these books reminded me of the things I *should* be doing. It reminded me of all the ways that I was failing in youth ministry.

It reminded me of all the charismatic leaders who have big personalities that are crushing the youth ministry game, and the reality that I simply was not crushing it.

I'm not a big personality or a hilarious speaker with 20,000 Instagram followers. I'm an introverted youth pastor who would rather read a book or watch football than play ultimate frisbee or go rock climbing (And I still have a job—crazy, I know).

And as I would think about these amazing leaders and think about the new ideas I should implement, I would remember the sermon I still needed to finish or the camp I hadn't started planning for. And in the midst of all this, I wouldn't add any new concepts that I had just read about.

There were many times these books left me discouraged and reminded me more of the ways I was losing, not the ways I was winning.

If there's one thing I want you to take away from this book, it's encouragement.

Whether you are a parent, teacher, pastor, or fill in the blank, be encouraged in the fact that the Creator of the Universe is using *you* to teach young people in your community the ways of Jesus.

For whatever reason, God did not hire the charismatic social media influencer to disciple the students at your church, He called *you*.

Gen Z doesn't need another influencer. They need someone who knows their name and loves them for who God created them to be.

So do not be discouraged when you put down this book, but be encouraged that God will accomplish His purposes through a faithful and humble servant.

Let us move with great passion and urgency for the advancement of the Kingdom in the lives of our young people. Let us lead, teach, listen, love, and pray that His Kingdom would come to Earth as it is in Heaven. But let us do all of this in light of the future reality—that our King will return and reign supreme for all eternity. Our future is secure. The hope of the world is still here. And God is up to something special with His young people.

So, no...The church won't end with Generation Z. Far from it.

ACKNOWLEDGMENTS

Someone once said, "It takes a village to raise a child." And while I've found this to be true with the recent birth of our first child, I would add that it takes a church to write a book. For me, the beautiful part of this book-writing journey has been the incorporation of all of the ideas, experiences, and lessons that I have learned from fellow Jesus followers. I could not have written this without them, so I want to spend some time highlighting those who have especially influenced my faith and my writing.

To my wife Alison, thank you for inspiring me, encouraging me, and believing in me. You were the first one who thought this was possible, and you supported me all the way through it (including the long nights of writing and editing with our baby Wesley)! I love you so, so much.

To my church family at Lake City, you mean the world to me. It is one of the great gifts of my life to pastor at this church. Thank you for allowing me this honor.

To my Kaleo fam, this book resembles so much of what I hope and dream of for you. Together we are on mission to see Jesus change the world through your generation. I love you all!

To my friends and family who read, edited, critiqued, and encouraged my writing, thank you! This book is more complete because of your help.

To Ron Marrs—who oversaw much of my studies at Western Seminary—thank you for walking alongside me in this research project. You are a Youth Ministry LEGEND!

Marty Michelson, you shaped much of my theological and pastoral convictions and wrote "I believe in you" letters to me during my undergraduate studies. Your belief in me as a student gave me the courage to take on a project like this. Thank you.

To my mentor Trevor Horn, your impact on my faith as a young person encouraged me to do the same for the young people in my life. I am grateful for your example and continued friendship.

And to the countless others who have walked alongside me in my faith journey, thank you. This book is what it is because of your influence.

ENDNOTES

Introduction

1. Matthew 16:18.

Chapter 1: We're Not in Kansas Anymore

1. Vidor, King, et al. *The Wizard of Oz*. Metro-Goldwyn-Mayer (MGM), 1939.

2. Hobbs, Frank, and Nicole Stoops. "Demographic Trends in the 20th Century - Census.gov." Census.gov, Nov. 2002, https://www.census.gov/prod/2002pubs/censr-4.pdf.

3. Tucker, Carol. "The 1950s - Powerful Years for Religion." *USC News*, 3 Apr. 2012, news.usc.edu/25835/The-1950s-Powerful-Years-for-Religion/.

4. Tucker, Carol. "The 1950s - Powerful Years for Religion."

5. Jones, Jeffrey M. "U.S. Church Membership Falls BELOW Majority for First Time." Gallup.com, Gallup, 13 Aug. 2021, news.gallup.com/poll/341963/church-membership-falls-below-majority-first-time.aspx.

6. Many researchers suggest the decline in Christianity is due to cultural Christians being more comfortable selecting "none" under religious affiliation. For more info check out: "Survey Fail - Christianity Isn't Dying: Ed Stetzer." *USA Today*, Gannett Satellite Information Network,

14 May 2015, https://www.usatoday.com/story/opinion/2015/05/13/nones-americans-christians-evangelicals-column/27198423/.

7. Ibid.

8. Napoli, Cassandra. "Zennials: The in-between Generation." WGSN, 21 May 2020, https://www.wgsn.com/insight/p/article/88103?lang=en.

9. Bentley, R. Alexander, et al. The Acceleration of Cultural Change: From Ancestors to Algorithms. The MIT Press, 2017.

10. Tanzola, Chuck. "'Toto, I've a Feeling We're Not in KANSAS Anymore' " Electronics Representatives Association." Electronics Representatives Association, 2020, era.org/toto-ive-a-feeling-were-not-in-kansas-anymore/.

11. Barna. Gen z. Barna Group, 2018.

12. Ibid.

Chapter 2: Introducing Z

1. Acts 13:36.

2. Psalm 78:1-4.

3. Karuhije, Benjamin. "3 Ways Gen Z Is Reshaping the Western Church." Identity Theology, 1 Feb. 2022, https://identitytheology.com/p/3-ways-gen-z-is-reshaping-the-western.

4. The exact dates on this vary. Sociologist Jean Twenge defines Gen Z as 1995-2012, while others consider the range to begin in 1996 or 1997.

5. Twenge, Jean M. Igen. Atria Books, 2017.

6. Parker, Kim, and Ruth Igielnik. "What We Know about Gen Z so Far." Pew Research Center's Social & Demographic Trends Project, Pew Research Center, 14 July 2021, https://www.pewresearch.org/social-trends/2020/05/14/on-the-cusp-of-adulthood-and-facing-an-uncertain-future-what-we-know-about-gen-z-so-far-2/.

7. "Feed.bible." Feed Youth Ministry, Oct. 2018, https://feed.bible/wp-content/uploads/2019/10/Gen-Z-Feed-Lit-Review.pdf.

8. Monster Worldwide, Inc. "Move over, millennials: Gen z Is about to Hit the Workforce." 29 June 2018,

9. Moore, Karl. "millennials Work for Purpose, Not Paycheck." *Forbes Magazine,* 3 Oct. 2014, https://www.forbes.com/sites/karlmoore/2014/10/02/millennials-work-for-purpose-not-paycheck/?sh=cc430886a51f.

10. Twenge, Jean M. *Igen.*

11. "Why America's 'Nones' Don't Identify with a Religion." Pew Research Center, Pew Research Center, 23 July 2020, https://www.pewresearch.org/fact-tank/2018/08/08/why-americas-nones-dont-identify-with-a-religion/.

12. "America's Changing Religious Landscape." Pew Research Center's Religion & Public Life Project, 12 Feb. 2021, www.pewforum.org/2015/05/12/americas-changing-religious-landscape/.

13. Barna puts this number at 64% while Lifeway records the number at 66%. In 2007 this number was at 70% according to Lifeway.

14. "Most Teenagers Drop out of Church When They Become Young Adults." Lifeway Research, 11 Aug. 2021, lifewayresearch.com/2019/01/15/most-teenagers-drop-out-of-church-as-young-adults/.

15. Ibid.

16. Consider the Prodigal Son in Luke 15:11-32 or God's use of Jonah despite Jonah's reluctance to obey.

17. Barna. "Meet Those Who 'Love Jesus but Not the Church.'" Barna Group, 2017, https://www.barna.com/research/meet-love-jesus-not-church/.

18. Ibid.

19. "Most Teenagers Drop out of Church When They Become Young Adults." Lifeway Research.

20. "Gen Z Is Keeping the Faith. Just Don't Expect to See Them at Worship." IFYC, 23 Sept. 2021, https://ifyc.org/article/gen-z-keeping-faith-just-dont-expect-see-them-worship.

21. Ibid.

22. 2 Corinthians 5:19.

23. Eph. 2:14-16.

24. Dever, Mark. "Why You Can't Be a Christian without the Church." Crossway, 23 Oct. 2020, www.crossway.org/articles/why-you-cant-be-a-christian-without-the-church/.

25. Villodas, Rich. Twitter, 27 July 2021, twitter.com/richvillodas/status/1375918691901186052?lang=ga.

26. Rom. 10:9-10.

Chapter 3: The Intersection of Church and Culture

1. Burnett, David, et al. Evangelical Dictionary of World Missions. Special Materials Services, Manitoba Education, 2007.

2. Conn, Harvie. "Culture" - Introducing World Missions. Baker Academic, 2000.

3. Consider Acts 17, where Paul communicates the Gospel to three different cultures. Also, the incarnation of Jesus is the most radical example of contextualization, where He literally took the form of the culture (man) yet was also divine.

4. 1 Corinthians 9:19–23.

5. Pratt, Zane. "Four Biblical Foundations for Contextualization." Originally written at Southeastern Seminary. Adapted from 9Marks, 18 July 2016, https://www.9marks.org/article/four-biblical-foundations-for-contextualization/.

6. Stetzer, Ed. "Proselytizing in a Multi-Faith World." ChristianityToday.com, *Christianity Today*, 28 Mar. 2011, https://www.christianitytoday.com/ct/2011/april/proselytizingmultifaith.html.

7. Gilliland, Dean S. *The Word Among Us: Contextualizing Theology for Mission Today*. Dallas: Word Pub, 1989.

8. Sánchez, Juan, et al. "To Contextualize or Not to Contextualize: That Is Not the Question." The Gospel Coalition, 13 Dec. 2009, https://www.thegospelcoalition.org/article/to-contextualize-or-not-to-contextualize-that-is-not-the-question/.

9. Bergler, Thomas E. "Generation Z and Spiritual Maturity." Christian Education Journal: Research on Educational Ministry, vol. 17, no. 1, 2020, pp. 75–91., https://doi.org/10.1177/0739891320903058.

10. Sittser, Gerald L. "The Early Church Thrived amid Secularism and Shows How We Can, Too." ChristianityToday.com, Christianity Today, 16 Oct. 2019, https://www.christianitytoday.com/ct/2019/october-web-only/early-church-thrived-amid-secularism-we-can-too.html.

11. Keller, Timothy J. Preaching: Communicating Faith in a Age of Skepticism. Viking, 2015.

12. Sayers, Mark. Disappearing Church: From Cultural Relevance to Gospel Resilience. Moody Publishers, 2016.

13. James 4:4.

14. Claiborne, Shane. The Irresistible Revolution: Living as an Ordinary Radical. Zondervan, 2016.

15. Matthew 28.

16. John 17:14.

17. Peterson, Galen. Contextualization. Taking the Gospel to Diverse Cultures, Western Seminary, Accessed 2021.

18. Stetzer, Ed. "Proselytizing in a Multi-Faith World." ChristianityToday. com, Christianity Today, 28 Mar. 2011, https://www.christianitytoday.com/ct/2011/april/proselytizingmultifaith.html.

19. Sayers, Mark. Disappearing Church.

20. While persecution doesn't always lead to church growth, the story of the early church was that it thrived despite public rejection.

21. Keller, Timothy J. Preaching.

Chapter 4: Reversing Culture: Back to Kansas?

1. Williamson, Pete. "Why I Voted for the Atheist President of HARVARD'S Chaplain Group." ChristianityToday.com, Christianity Today, 2 Sept. 2021, www.christianitytoday.com/ct/2021/september-web-only/atheism-harvard-interfaith-dialogue-why-i-voted-chaplain.html.

2. Cormode, Scott. *The Innovative church: How Leaders and Their Congregations Can Adapt in an Ever-Changing World.* Baker Academic, a Division of Baker Publishing Group, 2020.

3. Jeremiah 50:2

4. Jeremiah 29:4-7

5. "Religious Conservatives Imposing Their Views? A Reflection on the Ssm Debate - the Gospel Coalition: Australia." The Gospel Coalition | Australia, 10 Aug. 2017, au.thegospelcoalition.org/article/religious-con-servatives-imposing-their-views-a-reflection-on-the-ssm-debate/.

6. Mark 7:21-23

7. 2 Corinthians 5:17

8. KB. "KB HGA." Twitter, Twitter, 1 Nov. 2020, https://twitter.com/kb_hga/status/1322929460673470465.

9. Schleifer, James T. "Tocqueville, Religion, and Democracy in America, Some Essential Questions." American Political Thought, vol. 3, no. 2, The University of Chicago Press, 2014.

10. Inserra, Dean. "Will People Leave Your Church over Politics?" Lifeway Research, 10 Feb. 2021, lifewayresearch.com/2020/09/03/will-people-leave-your-church-over-american-politics/.

11. Nieuwhof, Carey. "8 Disruptive Church Trends That Will Rule 2021 (the Rise of the Post-Pandemic church)." CareyNieuwhof.com, 24 Aug. 2021, careynieuwhof.com/8-disruptive-church-trends-that-will-rule-2021-the-rise-of-the-post-pandemic-church/.

12. Hauerwas, Stanley Martin, and William Henry Willimon. Resident Aliens. Abingdon, 1989. Sittser, Gerald L. "The Early church Thrived amid Secularism and Shows How We Can, Too."

13. "Survey Fail - Christianity Isn't Dying: Ed Stetzer." *USA Today,* Gannett Satellite Information Network, 14 May 2015.

Chapter 5: The Conversation Starts With Us

1. Ferguson, Niall. The Great Degeneration. Penguin, 2014.

2. Sayers, Mark. Disappearing Church.

3. Ortlund, Ray, and Ray Ortlund (ThM. "Is Your Church an Institution?" The Gospel Coalition, 23 May 2017, https://www.thegospelcoalition.org/blogs/ray-ortlund/is-your-church-institution/.

4. Trueman, Carl R., and Rod Dreher. The Rise and Triumph of the Modern Self: Cultural Amnesia, Expressive Individualism, and the Road to Sexual Revolution. Crossway, 2020.

5. Matthew 7:3-5.

6. Consider Charles Taylor's A Secular Age.

7. Mark 10:42.

8. John 2:14-15.

9. "Why Did JESUS Get Angry and Flip Tables?" MattMcMillenMinistries.com, 3 Dec. 2020, mattmcmillenministries.com/why-did-jesus-get-angry-and-flip-tables/.

10. Mark 11:17.

11. Isaiah 56:4.

12. Isaiah 56:6.

13. Isaiah 56:8.

14. Cobb, Caroline, et al. "Would Jesus Turn over Tables in Today's Church?" The Gospel Coalition, 29 Apr. 2021, www.thegospelcoalition.org/article/jesus-turn-tables-church/.

15. James 3:1.

16. Vanderpool, Kurtis. "The Age of Deconstruction and Future of the church." RELEVANT, 7 Apr. 2021, www.relevantmagazine.com/faith/the-age-of-deconstruction-and-future-of-the-church/. .

17. Consider Acts 17:11, 1 John 4:1, and Proverbs 15:22

Chapter 6: Little Rascals and Horror Movies

1. "Millennial." Urban Dictionary, https://www.urbandictionary.com/define.php?term=Millennial.

2. Kinnaman, David, and Aly Hawkins. You Lost Me: Why Young Christians Are Leaving Church ... and Rethinking Faith. Baker Books, 2016.

3. Barna. "Six Reasons Young Christians Leave church." Barna Group, www.barna.com/research/six-reasons-young-christians-leave-church/.

4. Kinnaman, David, and Gabe Lyons. Unchristian: What a New Generation Really Thinks about Christianity—and Why It Matters. Baker Book House, 2012.

5. Barna Group. The State of YOUTH Ministry: How Churches Reach Today's Teens--and What Parents Think about It. a Barna Report Produced in Partnership with Youth Specialties and YouthWorks, 2016.

6. Romans 5:3; Galatians 2:20-21.

7. 2 Corinthians 12:10.

8. Wang, Yan & Dogan, Enis & Lin, Xiaodong. (2006). The effect of multiple-perspective thinking on problem solving. ICLS 2006 - International Conference of the Learning Sciences, Proceedings. 2. 812-817.

9. Barna. Gen z. Barna Group, 2018.

10. Rosin, Hanna. "The Overprotected Kid." The Atlantic, Atlantic Media Company, 16 Apr. 2018, www.theatlantic.com/magazine/archive/2014/04/hey-parents-leave-those-kids-alone/358631/.

11. Gage, Beverly. "America Is Safer than It Used to Be. so Why Do We Still Have Calls for 'Law and Order'?" The New York Times, The New York Times, 30 Aug. 2016, https://www.nytimes.com/2016/09/04/magazine/america-is-safer-than-it-used-to-be-so-why-do-we-still-have-calls-for-law-and-order.html.

12. Kristian, Bonnie. "Fear, Crime, and the Christian Response." Christianity Today, Oct. 2021.

13. Rosin, Hanna. "The Overprotected Kid."

14. Lythcott-Haims, Julie. How to Raise an Adult: Break Free of the Overparenting Trap and Prepare Your Kid for Success. Saint Martin's Griffin, 2016.

15. Twenge, Jean M. Igen. 2017.

16. Haberman, Clyde. "How an Abstinence Pledge in the '90s Shamed a Generation of Evangelicals." The New York Times, 6 Apr. 2021, www.nytimes.com/2021/04/06/us/abstinence-pledge-evangelicals.html.

17. Lewis, C. S. The Lion, the Witch, and the Wardrobe. Geoffrey Bless, 1950.

18. Matt. 10:22

19. John 15:20

20. Claiborne, Shane. The Irresistible Revolution: Living as an Ordinary Radical. Zondervan, 2016.

Chapter 7: System Students

1. FOX Sports. "The Top 10 College Football Players of All Time Ranked – and Why Cam Newton Is No. 1." FOX Sports, FOX Sports, 14 June 2021, www.foxsports.com/stories/college-football/rj-young-heisman-trophy-greatest-cfb-players-ever-cam-newton-reggie-bush-vince-young.

2. Matt 28:18-20.

3. Ephesians 4:12

4. Acts 2:44-46

5. Powell, Kara, director Kara Powell on the #1 Reason Youth Leave the Church—And How to Reverse the Trend. church Leaders Podcast, 2021. Podcast, Accessed 2021.

6. 1 Corinthians 1:2

7. Vanderstelt, Jeff. Saturate: Being Disciples of Jesus in the Everyday Stuff of Life. Crossway, 2015.

8. 1 Timothy 1:2

9. "5 Ways to Connect with millennials." Barna Group, 9 Sept. 2014, www.barna.com/research/5-ways-to-connect-with-millennials/.

10. Clark, Chap. Adoptive Youth Ministry: Integrating Emerging Generations into the Family of Faith. Baker Academic, a Division of Baker Publishing Group, 2016.

Chapter 8: Be Real, Bro

1. Francis, Tracy, and Fernanda Hoefel. "'True Gen': Generation z and Its Implications for Companies." *McKinsey & Company,* McKinsey & Company, 16 Dec. 2020, www.mckinsey.com/industries/consumer-packaged-goods/our-insights/true-gen-generation-z-and-its-implications-for-companies.

2. Dugan, Mary Ellen. "Gen z Doesn't Want to Buy Your Brand, They Want to Join It." *Ad Age,* 15 Apr. 2019, adage.com/article/wp-engine/gen-z-doesnt-want-buy-your-brand-they-want-join-it/2163281.

3. Carr, Sam. "How Many Ads Do We See a Day? 2021 Daily Ad Exposure Revealed." *PPC Protect,* 18 Aug. 2021, ppcprotect.com/how-many-ads-do-we-see-a-day/.

4. O'Brien, Brandon. "Explainer: The Micro CHURCH Movement." *CT Pastors,* Leadership Journal, 24 July 2009, www.christianitytoday.com/pastors/2009/july-online-only/explainer-micro-church-movement.html.

5. Nieuwhof, Carey. "Why Cool Church Doesn't Work Anymore (More on the Future church)." CareyNieuwhof.com, 28 June 2021, careynieuwhof.com/why-cool-church-doesnt-work-anymore-more-on-the-future-church/.

6. Shane Sanchez, et al. "3 Foundational Principles for Next-Gen Ministry." OutreachMagazine.com, 13 Oct. 2020, outreachmagazine.com/features/leadership/60479-3-foundational-principles-for-next-gen-ministry.html.

7. Pruitt, Shane. "Gen Z…" Twitter, Twitter, 10 Sept. 2021, twitter.com/shane_pruitt78/status/1436373644268163072.

8. McCracken, Brett. *Hipster Christianity: When Church and Cool Collide.* Baker Books, 2010.

9. Bevins, Winfield. "Something Old, Something New: How New Churches Are Embracing Liturgy." *Azusa Pacific University,* vol. 11, no. 2, 2020.

10. Ibid.

11. Evans, Rachel Held. "Want millennials Back in the Pews? Stop Trying to Make Church 'Cool.'." *The Washington Post,* WP Company, 30 Apr. 2015, www.washingtonpost.com/opinions/jesus-doesnt-tweet/2015/04/30/fb07ef1a-ed01-11e4-8666-a1d756d0218e_story.html.

12. Bevins, Winfield. "Something Old, Something New: How New Churches Are Embracing Liturgy."

13. Barna. "Designing Worship Spaces with millennials in Mind." *Barna Group,* 5 Nov. 2014, https://www.barna.com/research/designing-worship-spaces-with-millennials-in-mind/.

14. Samuel, Stephanie. "Study Shows millennials Turned off by Trendy church Buildings, Prefer a Classic Sanctuary." *The Christian Post,* Nov. 2014, https://www.christianpost.com/news/study-shows-millennials-turned-off-by-trendy-church-buildings-prefer-a-classic-sanctuary.html.

15. John 8:34-36.

16. Genesis 3:8.

17. Schieber, Hamutal. "Creators and Content Are the Future of Gen z and Brand Interaction." *Schieber Research,* researchci.com/creators-and-content-are-the-future-of-gen-z-and-brand-interaction/.

18. Ibid.

19. "A Quote from the Office." The Office Quotes, http://www.theofficequotes.com/season-3/business-school/quote_1224.

20. Pokluda, Jonathan. *Welcoming the Future church: How to Reach, Teach, and Engage Young Adults.* Baker Books, a Division of Baker Publishing Group, 2020.

21. "About The Porch." *About | ThePorch.Live,* Watermark, https://www.theporch.live/about.

22. Pokluda, Jonathan. *Welcoming the Future Church.*

Chapter 9: The Present is King

1. Livermore, David *A Cultural Intelligence: Improving Your Cq to Engage Our Multicultural World.* Baker Academic, 2009.

2. Hebrews 13:8

3. Landrum, Tessa. "Gen z Is Spiritually Illiterate and Abandoning church: How Did We Get Here?" Kentucky Today, Kentucky Today, 9 July 2020, www.kentuckytoday.com/stories/gen-z-is-spiritually-illiterate-and-abandoning-the-church-how-did-we-get-here,23397.

4. 1 Cor. 15:14

5. Kinnaman, David, et al. *Faith for EXILES: 5 Ways for a New Generation to Follow Jesus in DIGITAL Babylon.* Baker Books, a Division of Baker Publishing Group, 2019.

6. Exodus 16; 32

7. See Exodus 20:2, 29:6; Deut. 5:6.

8. Piper, John, and John Piper. *Future Grace: The Purifying Power of the Promises of God.* Multnomah Books, 2012.

9. Wilhoit, Jim. *Spiritual Formation as If the church Mattered: Growing in Christ through Community.* Baker Academic, a Division of Baker Publishing Group, 2008.

10. Haberer, Jack. *Living the Presence of the Spirit.* Geneva Press, 2001.

Chapter 10: Hurt

1. "Five Reasons People Leave the Church." *Your Move,* https://your-move.is/five-reasons-people-leave-the-church/.

2. "Six Reasons Young Christians Leave Church." *Barna Group,* 2011, https://www.barna.com/research/six-reasons-young-christians-leave-church/.

3. Ibid.

4. Ibid.

5. Capitides, Christina. "A Cup Full of Spit, a Chewed up Piece of Gum. These Are the Metaphors Used to Teach Kids about Sex." CBS News, CBS Interactive, 29 Apr. 2019, https://www.cbsnews.com/news/a-cup-full-of-spit-a-chewed-up-piece-of-gum-these-are-the-metaphors-used-to-teach-kids-about-sex/.

6. 1 John 4:18.

7. LGBTQ is an acronym for lesbian, gay, bisexual, transgender and queer or questioning. The acronym is often followed by a "+" to indicate other communities not included in the acronym.

8. Jones, Jeffrey M. "LGBT Identification Rises to 5.6% in Latest U.S. Estimate." Gallup.com, Gallup, 20 Nov. 2021, https://news.gallup.com/poll/329708/lgbt-identification-rises-latest-estimate.aspx.

9. Kinnaman, David, and Gabe Lyons. *Unchristian: What a New Generation Really Thinks about Christianity—and Why It Matters*. Baker Book House, 2012.

10. Jones, Robert Patrick. *The End of White Christian America*. Simon & Schuster, 2017.

11. Jones, Robert P. "Exodus: Why Americans Are Leaving Religion-and Why They're Unlikely to Come Back." PRRI, 15 Oct. 2021, https://www.prri.org/research/prri-rns-poll-nones-atheist-leaving-religion/.

12. Marin, Andrew P. *US versus Us: The Untold Story of Religion and the LGBT Community*. The Navigators, 2016.

13. Other reasons for LGBTQ people leaving the church include, "Unwillingness to dialogue "(12%) and "Kicked out" (9%).

14. Marin, Andrew P. *US versus Us*.

15. This data is from Barna's You Lost Me, by David Kinnaman.

16. Other answers include "No attempts to change their sexual orientation" (6%), "Authenticity" (5%), and "Support of family and friends" (4%).

17. John 10:10.

18. I came across this analogy from Elizabeth Esther on her website: Elizabethesther.com.

19. 1 Corinthians 12:26.

20. Galatians 6:2.

21. Colossians 3:12.

Chapter 11: A Catalyst Called Doubt

1. Powell, Kara. "I Doubt It." *Fuller Youth Institute*, 2014, fulleryouthinstitute.org/blog/i-doubt-it.

2. "Six Reasons Young Christians Leave church."

3. Ibid.

4. Huckabee, Tyler. "How Gen z Will Shape the church." RELEVANT, 7 Sept. 2021, www.relevantmagazine.com/magazine/how-gen-z-will-shape-the-church/.

5. Anderson, Janna, and Lee Rainie. "The Future of Truth and Misinformation Online." Pew Research Center: Internet, Science & Tech, Pew Research Center, 17 Aug. 2020, https://www.pewresearch.org/internet/2017/10/19/the-future-of-truth-and-misinformation-online/.

6. Kastenholz, Christoph. "Council Post: Gen Z and the Rise of Social Commerce." Forbes, *Forbes Magazine,* 10 Dec. 2021, https://www.forbes.com/sites/forbesagencycouncil/2021/05/17/gen-z-and-the-rise-of-social-commerce/?sh=20b69338251d.

7. Barna. Gen z. Barna Group, 2018.

8. Powell, Kara, director. The #1 Reason Youth Leave the Church. Church Leaders Podcast, June 2021.

9. Matt. 11:28.

10. John 20:24-25.

11. John 20:28.

12. Maier, Paul. Eusebius - The Church History. Stl, 2007.

13. Still, Jay. The New Testament Historical Enrichment Book. Author Solutions, Incorporated, 2014.

14. McDowell, Sean. "Did the Apostle Thomas Die as a Martyr?" Sean McDowell, 25 Feb. 2016, seanmcdowell.org/blog/did-the-apostle-thomas-die-as-a-martyr. Another good source is: Still, Jay. The New Testament Historical Enrichment Book. Author Solutions, Incorporated, 2014.

Chapter 12: Killing the Brand

1. Wilkens, Steve, and Mark L. Sanford. Hidden Worldviews: Eight Cultural Stories That Shape Our Lives. Distributed by Amazon Digital Services, 2012.

2. "Consumerism Definition & Meaning." Merriam-Webster, Merriam-Webster, https://www.merriam-webster.com/dictionary/consumerism.

3. McDannell, Colleen. Material Christianity: Religion and Popular Culture in America. Yale Univ. Press, 1995.

4. Engelkemier, Joe. "A Church That Draws Thousands." Ministry Magazine, May 1991, www.ministrymagazine.org/archive/1991/05/a-church-that-draws-thousands.

5. Jones, Robert Patrick. The End of White Christian America. Simon & Schuster, 2017.

6. William Lobdell and Mitchell Landsberg, "Rev. Robert H. Schuller, who built Crystal Cathedral, dies at 88," The Los Angeles Times, April 2, 2015.

7. Luecke, David S. "Is Willow Creek the Way of the Future?" Religion Online, 1 May 1997, www.religion-online.org/article/is-willow-creek-the-way-of-the-future/.

8. McKnight, Scot, et al. "The Legacy of Willow Creek 2." Jesus Creed | A Blog by Scot McKnight, 6 Oct. 2020, www.christianitytoday.com/scot-mcknight/2020/october/legacy-of-willow-creek-2.html.

9. Rainey, Russ. "Willow Creek Reveal Study – a Summary - the Christian Coaching Center." The Christian Coaching Center Willow Creek Reveal Study a Summary Comments, http://www.christiancoachingcenter.org/index.php/russ-rainey/coachingchurch2/.

10. Editorial, A Christianity Today. "Editorial: What Willow's Reveal Reveals." ChristianityToday.com, Christianity Today, 27 Feb. 2008, https://www.christianitytoday.com/ct/2008/march/11.27.html.

11. Matthew 4:4.

12. Samuel, Stephanie. "Francis Chan: Church Wastes Too Much Time Waiting on God's Voice; Christians Getting Too Fat on the Word." The Christian Post, 28 Feb. 2015, www.christianpost.com/news/francis-chan-church-wastes-too-much-time-waiting-on-gods-voice-christians-getting-too-fat-on-the-word.html.

13. Philippians 4:9.

14. Barna. "Meet Those Who 'Love Jesus but Not the church.'" Barna Group, 30 Mar. 2017, www.barna.com/research/meet-love-jesus-not-church/.

15. Luke 11:37-44 describes Jesus' "woes" against the pharisees who knew the small intricacies of Scripture yet failed to love their neighbor.

16. Dugan, Mary Ellen. "Gen Z Doesn't Want to Buy Your Brand, They Want to Join It." Ad Age.

17. Premack, Rachel. "Gen Zs Never Watch TV, Are Stressed about Snapchat, and Are Concerned That Technology Has Ruined Their Mental Health - Here's What It's Really like to Be a Teen." Business Insider, Business Insider, 29 June 2018, www.businessinsider.com/teens-gen-z-generation-z-what-teens-are-like-2018-6.

18. Mack, Maddie. "Culture Creators: Catalysts of Cultural Revolution: Infographic." Lemonly, The Wildness, 2015, lemonly.com/work/culture-creators-infographic-report.

19. Hatzipanagos, Rachel. "Gen Z Is Making Change, One Protest at a Time." The Washington Post, WP Company, 12 Mar. 2021, https://www.washingtonpost.com/nation/2021/03/15/gen-z-is-making-change-one-protest-time/.

20. Ibid.

21. Savage, Jon. Teenage: The Prehistory of Youth Culture, 1875-1945. Penguin Books, 2008.

22. Gandio, Del. Rhetoric for Radicals a Handbook for Twenty-First Century Activists. New Society Pub, 2008.

23. Alyssa Biederman, Melina Walling. "Meet Gen Z Activists: Called to Action in an Unsettled World." AP NEWS, Associated Press, 29 Sept. 2020, https://apnews.com/article/climate-race-and-ethnicity-shootings-climate-change-school-violence-01673bd21da246ce942d1e98a08fc96f.

24. Kristof, Nicholas. "Is the Business World All About Greed?" The New York Times, The New York Times, 24 Jan. 2018, https://www.nytimes.com/2018/01/24/opinion/davos-corporate-social-impact.html.

25. Patel, Deep. "Gen Z Hates TV, and What That Means for Traditional Advertising." Forbes, Forbes Magazine, 30 May 2017, https://www.forbes.com/sites/deeppatel/2017/05/30/gen-z-hates-tv-and-what-that-means-for-traditional-advertising/?sh=2a986d0332ed.

26. Burgess, Eric. "Social Media Creators Are More Influential than Celebrities." [ION], 22 Aug. 2016, https://www.ion.co/millennials-listen-social-media-creators-celebrities.

27. CommScope. "CommScope Research on Gen Z Tech Intimates." CommScope, 2017, www.commscope.com/press-releases/2017/commscope-research-on-gen-z-tech-intimates-reveals-an-always-on-mindset/.

28. Nieuwhof, Carey. "6 Characteristics of an Irrelevant Leader." CareyNieuwhof.com, 26 Nov. 2019, careynieuwhof.com/6-characteristics-of-an-irrelevant-leader/.

29. Matt. 28:19-20.

30. Mark 12:30-31.

31. Colossians 3:23.

32. Matthew 6:10.

33. Matthew 24:14.

Chapter 13: Engaging ~~Consumers~~ Creators

1. "Life.Church Locations." Home, https://www.life.church/locations/.

2. This came from a talk I heard Vince give a few years ago.

3. Ephesians 4:11-12.

4. Matt. 20:26-28.

5. I first heard this analogy from my time at Life.church.

6. "Growing Young (Online Site)." Fuller Youth Institute, https://fulleryouthinstitute.org/growingyoung.

7. Powell, Kara Eckmann. Growing Young: Six Essential Strategies to Help Young People Discover and Love Your church.

8. Dodd, Rachel. "5 Steps to Practice Keychain Leadership with Students." Fuller Youth Institute, 24 Oct. 2019, fulleryouthinstitute.org/blog/5-steps-to-practice-keychain-leadership-with-students.

9. If you've never heard of the Jesus Movement, it was an incredible revival amongst young people starting on the West Coast.

10. Needham, Nick R. 2000 Years of Christ's Power. Christian Focus Publications Ltd, 2016.

11. "The Bible App". YouVersion. Retrieved October 30, 2020.

12. Cormode, Scott. The Innovative church: How Leaders and Their Congregations Can Adapt in an Ever-Changing World.

13. Life.church. "Faith-Filled, Big-Thinking." Talk It Over, www.life.church/talkitover/jesus-and-we-1/.

14. "Youversion Bible App." YouVersion, 4 Nov. 2021, https://www.youversion.com/the-bible-app/.

15. Jaradat, Mya. "Gen Z's Looking for Religion. You'd Be Surprised Where They Find It." Deseret News, Deseret News, 14 Sept. 2020, https://www.deseret.com/indepth/2020/9/13/21428404/gen-z-religion-spirituality-social-justice-black-lives-matter-parents-family-pandemic.

16. Ibid.

17. Hudson, Hugh, Colin Welland, and David Puttnam. Chariots of Fire. London: Enigma Productions, 1981.

18. Wilhoit, Jim. Spiritual Formation as If the Church Mattered. 2008.

19. Kelly, James. "Learning Pyramid." The Peak Performance Center, Sept. 2012, thepeakperformancecenter.com/educational-learning/learning/principles-of-learning/learning-pyramid/.

20. Kelly, James. "Learning Pyramid."

21. Bachelor, Robin L. "Exploring the Effects of Active Learning on Retaining Essential Concepts in Secondary and Junior High Classrooms." Saint Xavier University, 2012.

22. McSpadden, Kevin. "Science: You Now Have a Shorter Attention Span than a Goldfish." Time, Time, 14 May 2015, https://time.com/3858309/attention-spans-goldfish/.

23. Crary, David. "How Long Is the Sermon? Study Ranks Christian Churches." AP NEWS, Associated Press, 16 Dec. 2019, https://apnews.com/article/us-news-ap-top-news-religion-christianity-d5c3a0bd7726f18d-5cff44efa1bd4cfd.

24. Leeman, Jonathan. "How Long Should a Sermon Be?" 9Marks, 2020, https://www.9marks.org/article/how-long-should-a-sermon-be/.

25. Stanley, Andy, et al. Communicating for a Change: Seven Keys to Irresistible Communication. Multnomah, 2006.

Chapter 14: Changes

1. Shakur, Tupac. "2Pac (Ft. Talent) – Changes." Genius, https://genius.com/2pac-changes-lyrics.

2. "Suicide Statistics." American Foundation for Suicide Prevention, American Foundation for Suicide Prevention, 9 Sept. 2021, https://afsp.org/suicide-statistics/.

3. Nieuwhof, Carey. "Cheat Sheet: 13 Facts about Change Many Leaders Don't Realize." CareyNieuwhof.com, 29 July 2013, https://careynieuwhof.com/cheat-sheet-13-facts-about-change-many-leaders-dont-realize/.

4. Exodus 3:13.

Chapter 15: The Future Church

1. Bailey, Sarah Pulliam. "The World Is Expected to Become More Religious - Not Less." The Washington Post, WP Company, 24 Apr. 2015, https://www.washingtonpost.com/news/acts-of-faith/wp/2015/04/24/the-world-is-expected-to-become-more-religious-not-less/.

2. Woo, (Photo: Reuters/Jon. "China on Track to Have World's Largest Christian Population by 2030." The Christian Post, 16 July 2016, https://www.christianpost.com/news/china-largest-christian-population-world-200-million-believers-despite-crackdown.html.

3. "10 Encouraging Trends of Global Christianity in 2020." Lifeway Research, 18 Jan. 2022, https://research.lifeway.com/2020/06/10/10-encouraging-trends-of-global-christianity-in-2020/.

4. "7 Surprising Trends in Global Christianity in 2019." Lifeway Research, 17 Dec. 2021, https://research.lifeway.com/2019/06/11/7-surprising-trends-in-global-christianity-in-2019/.

5. "10 Encouraging Trends of Global Christianity in 2020." Lifeway Research.

6. Keller, Timothy. Making Sense of God: Finding God in the Modern World. Penguin Books, 2018.

7. Kiersz, Andy. "Suicide Is Gen Z's Second-Leading Cause of Death, and It's a Worse Epidemic than Anything millennials Faced at That Age." Business Insider, Business Insider, 17 Oct. 2019, https://www.businessinsider.com/cdc-teenage-gen-z-american-suicide-epidemic.

8. Isaiah 9:2.

9. I first heard this from Craig Groeschel of Life.church.

57074573R00144